Abortion & Pregnancy Options

Editor: Danielle Lobban

Volume 438

independence
educational publishers

Acknowledgements

The publisher is grateful for permission to reproduce the material in this book. While every care has been taken to trace and acknowledge copyright, the publisher tenders its apology for any accidental infringement or where copyright has proved untraceable. The publisher would be pleased to come to a suitable arrangement in any such case with the rightful owner.

The material reproduced in **issues** books is provided as an educational resource only. The views, opinions and information contained within reprinted material in **issues** books do not necessarily represent those of Independence Educational Publishers and its employees.

Images

Cover image courtesy of iStock. All other images courtesy of Freepik, Pixabay and Unsplash.

Additional acknowledgements

With thanks to the Independence team: Shelley Baldry, Tracy Biram, Klaudia Sommer and Jackie Staines.

Danielle Lobban

Cambridge, January 2024

Contents

Introduction

Abortion & Pregnancy Options is Volume 438 in the **issues** series. The aim of the series is to offer current, diverse information about important issues in our world, from a UK perspective.

About Abortion & Pregnancy Options

In the UK 25% of pregnancies end by termination. This book explores the options available in the event of an unplanned pregnancy such as abortion or adoption. It also looks at legislation on reproductive rights around the world, the impact on women's health, and views from both the pro-choice and pro-life lobbies.

Our sources

Titles in the **issues** series are designed to function as educational resource books, providing a balanced overview of a specific subject.

The information in our books is comprised of facts, articles and opinions from many different sources, including:

- Newspaper reports and opinion pieces
- Website factsheets
- Magazine and journal articles
- Statistics and surveys
- Government reports
- Literature from special interest groups.

A note on critical evaluation

Because the information reprinted here is from a number of different sources, readers should bear in mind the origin of the text and whether the source is likely to have a particular bias when presenting information (or when conducting their research). It is hoped that, as you read about the many aspects of the issues explored in this book, you will critically evaluate the information presented.

It is important that you decide whether you are being presented with facts or opinions. Does the writer give a biased or unbiased report? If an opinion is being expressed, do you agree with the writer? Is there potential bias to the 'facts' or statistics behind an article?

Activities

Throughout this book, you will find a selection of assignments and activities designed to help you engage with the articles you have been reading and to explore your own opinions. Some tasks will take longer than others and there is a mixture of design, writing and research-based activities that you can complete alone or in a group.

Further research

At the end of each article we have listed its source and a website that you can visit if you would like to conduct your own research. Please remember to critically evaluate any sources that you consult and consider whether the information you are viewing is accurate and unbiased.

Issues Online

The **issues** series of books is complemented by our online resource, issuesonline.co.uk

On the Issues Online website you will find a wealth of information, covering over 70 topics, to support the PSHE and RSE curriculum.

Why Issues Online?

Researching a topic? Issues Online is the best place to start for...

Librarians

Issues Online is an essential tool for librarians: feel confident you are signposting safe, reliable, user-friendly online resources to students and teaching staff alike. We provide multi-user concurrent access, so no waiting around for another student to finish with a resource. Issues Online also provides FREE downloadable posters for your shelf/wall/ table displays.

Teachers

Issues Online is an ideal resource for lesson planning, inspiring lively debate in class and setting lessons and homework tasks.

Our accessible, engaging content helps deepen students' knowledge, promotes critical thinking and develops independent learning skills.

Issues Online saves precious preparation time. We wade through the wealth of material on the internet to filter the best quality, most relevant and up-to-date information you need to start exploring a topic.

Our carefully selected, balanced content presents an overview and insight into each topic from a variety of sources and viewpoints.

Students

Issues Online is designed to support your studies in a broad range of topics, particularly social issues relevant to young people today.

Thousands of articles, statistics and infographs instantly available to help you with research and assignments.

With 24/7 access using the powerful Algolia search system, you can find relevant information quickly, easily and safely anytime from your laptop, tablet or smartphone, in class or at home.

Visit issuesonline.co.uk to find out more!

Making a decision about a pregnancy

There are many different reasons why people get abortions, and all of them are valid. Find out more about deciding whether or not to have an abortion.

If you are pregnant you have three basic choices:

Choice A: go through with the pregnancy and become a parent.

Choice B: go through with the pregnancy and place the baby for adoption.

Choice C: end the pregnancy by having an abortion.

How do you feel about being pregnant?

In order to decide what you want to do, it is important to think about how you feel about being pregnant. Perhaps you planned to get pregnant because you wanted to have a baby, and that is still what you want most at this time. If so, you will probably decide on Choice A – continuing the pregnancy and keeping the baby.

If that is no longer what you want, or if you didn't intend to get pregnant in the first place, you can start by looking more closely at how you feel about being pregnant. An unintended pregnancy can arouse many different feelings. In fact, most people find they have mixed or conflicting feelings.

For example, you might feel:

* Worried about being able to manage a baby
* Afraid you'll have to give up other things that are important to you
* Concerned about how other people may react

At the same time you may also feel:

* Happy to learn that you can get pregnant
* Pleased to have the opportunity to have a baby
* Excited by a new and unique event in your life

It might help to list the different feelings you have right now about being pregnant.

What are your hopes and plans for the future?

It is also important to think about what you want from your future. Here are some good questions to ask yourself about your life right now and about your future:

* What are two or three things that matter most to me in my life right now?
* What are two or three things that I hope to have or achieve in the next five to ten years?

In order to achieve those things:

* How would having a baby help?
* How would adoption help?
* How would abortion help?

What would I lose or give up right now:

* If I have a baby?
* If I place the baby for adoption?
* If I have an abortion?

What are your beliefs?

Up to this point, you've been looking at the possible effects of different decisions on your plans and dreams. Now look at your thoughts, values, and beliefs about your situation and the different choices.

Following are some statements people often make. Check the ones that fit for you, and write in other thoughts you have.

Choice A: having a baby and keeping it

- I feel ready to take on the tasks of being a parent
- Some people have said they will help me
- I want a child more than I want anything else
- My partner and I both want to have a baby
- I think I am too young (or too old) to have a baby
- I don't believe I can manage to raise a child properly
- Having a child now would stop me from having the life I want for myself
- I don't feel ready to take on the tasks of being a parent

Choice B: having a baby and putting it up for adoption

- I could continue the pregnancy and give birth, without having to raise the child
- I could help the child have parents who want it and can care for it
- I could postpone being a parent myself until later in my life when I feel ready

- I like the idea of giving someone else the baby they can't create themselves
- I don't think I could give up the baby after nine months of pregnancy and delivery
- I would not like living with the idea that someone else has my baby
- I would worry about whether the baby was being well treated. My family would rather have the baby stay in the family than go to strangers

Choice C: having an abortion

- I would like to postpone being a parent until my situation is better (older, finished school, more financially secure, in a stable relationship)
- I don't want to be a single parent
- My partner doesn't want a baby, and I want to consider their feelings
- An abortion is a safe and sensible way to take care of an unwanted pregnancy
- My religious beliefs are against abortion
- I would not like living with the idea that someone else has my baby
- I'm afraid I might not be able to get pregnant again
- My family (or someone else who is important to me) opposes abortion

Choosing to get an abortion

If you don't want to have a baby, or go through with an adoption, you can choose to have an abortion. People choose to end a pregnancy for lots of reasons. It might be because they don't want children, or aren't financially able to support a child. It might also be because it would be medically unsafe for them to have a baby. Whatever someone's reasons are for having an abortion, it is their choice and their right to do so.

The only person who can decide whether an abortion is right for you is you. It's really important to remember that the decision is up to you, because lots of people have very strong views about abortion – whether it's right or wrong – but none of them are you, and it's your choice.

Lots of people are against abortion, because of moral or religious views. They have a right to be against it, but they don't have a right to force other people to think the same way, or to stop anyone from getting an abortion.

People who are against abortion often say that it has bad effects on the people who have them – for example, they say abortion causes mental health problems, or that people who have abortions find it harder or impossible to get pregnant in the future. This isn't true. Lots of studies have found that abortion does not cause long-term mental health problems, or problems with getting pregnant. There's no link between abortion and breast cancer, either.

Even though one in three women in the UK will have an abortion during her lifetime, many people who have had an abortion don't talk about it. But you almost certainly know someone who has had an abortion, even if they haven't told you that they have.

Some people are very clear about their decision to have an abortion. Some people find it really hard, and might take some time to make up their mind. Either way, it's really important to be sure of your decision. You can talk to other people to help you decide – your friends, a family member, a counsellor, your partner – but in the end it has to be your decision. No one can make you have an abortion if you don't want to, and no one has the right to force you to stay pregnant if it's not what you want.

It's OK to have different emotions about having an abortion, too. Because some people have strong anti-abortion feelings, sometimes people who have them feel like they are doing something wrong. At Brook we believe that abortion is not bad or wrong. We think anyone who has decided to have an abortion should be treated without judgement, because it is their decision.

People from all walks of life have abortions every day for every reason imaginable. Sometimes, even people who are against abortion might decide to have an abortion if they get pregnant and don't want to be – and that's OK too. Everyone has the right to choose and everyone has the right to confidential and safe medical treatment.

Talking it over

Whether the decision to have an abortion is simple or hard for you, you can talk it over with someone you trust if you want to.

If you're going to ask a friend or family member for advice, please make sure you trust them completely, because if you want it kept a secret (which is your right), you don't want them telling other friends or people you know. It's fine to want to keep your decision private.

You can have an abortion without your parents' or carers' permission, even if you are under 16 years of age. Some people can talk to their parents about their decision to have an abortion and can get support from them. Some people don't want to tell their parents, because they are afraid of what they might say, or because they don't want their parents to know they had sex. You don't have to tell them if you don't want to.

If you are in a relationship, you might want to talk to your partner about your options. It is up to you. But even if your partner is the person who you became pregnant with, that doesn't mean they can tell you what decision to make. It's your body and your choice.

There are specially trained counsellors who can give you a chance to talk about your decision. If you go to your GP, you can ask to be referred to a counsellor. The charities British Pregnancy Advisory Service (BPAS) and MSI Reproductive Choices UK have counsellors you can talk to before an abortion. Their counsellors are pro-choice – that is, they will not push you to have an abortion, or to continue with the pregnancy. They will listen to you and help you come to a decision, but the decision will be yours.

Crisis Pregnancy Centres

If you are looking for support around making a decision, be careful as some places pretend to offer impartial and unbiased advice, but actually they use counselling to persuade people not to have abortions. Sometimes they tell people that having an abortion is linked to breast cancer, or mental health problems – neither of which is true.

These places are called crisis pregnancy centres, and when Brook investigated them, we found they were trying to make up people's minds for them, rather than helping them make their own decision.

Finding support

Brook services do not perform abortions but we do provide emergency contraception, pregnancy tests and abortion referrals. This means that Brook can provide you with emergency contraception, pregnancy tests, and if you are pregnant and want to end the pregnancy – we can refer and support you into other services near you that provide abortions.

19 January 2021

Roe vs Wade: 'Adoption is not an alternative to abortion – my pregnancy was harrowing and I wanted my baby'

The argument that adoption renders abortion unnecessary was made by the US Supreme Court.

By Connie Dimsdale

'Pregnancy was a harrowing undertaking even though I wanted to have the baby,' said one mother in response to the argument that women should put their newborn up for adoption rather than getting an abortion.

The argument is often made in pro-life circles in the US. In December last year, Supreme Court Judge Amy Coney Barrett – who is an adoptive mother herself – said that adoption renders abortion unnecessary as it protects women from 'forced motherhood'.

The argument also appeared around halfway through the US Supreme Court's 98-page draft majority opinion written by Justice Samuel Alito and published by Politico in May, which suggested the court would strike down the Roe v Wade ruling.

Today, the US Supreme Court has done just that. It voted to overturn the nationwide legal right to abortion in America, paving the way for individual states to heavily restrict or even ban the procedure.

The decision is expected to lead to abortion bans in roughly half of America's 50 states.

Back in May, when the draft opinion was leaked, protests erupted across the world against the plans to overturn Roe v Wade – a 1973 landmark ruling which protects the constitutional right to have an abortion.

One section of the opinion asserted that 'modern developments', including 'safe haven' laws which allow parents to anonymously give up babies without legal repercussions, mean that abortion is less necessary.

Abortion rights groups say this argument reduces the experience of pregnancy and giving birth as nothing more than nine months of inconvenience.

But for PhD candidate Abbie Heffer, who lives in Stuttgart, Germany, it was a 'horrific ordeal', even though she wanted to be pregnant and was excited about motherhood.

Ms Heffer, 30, experienced severe 'all-day sickness' for the first six months of her pregnancy then, just when she started feeling better with two months to go, she fractured her pelvis.

Actually giving birth was enjoyable, she said, but the afterbirth process almost killed her, as the placenta would not detach. The emergency on-call doctor treating her had to pull it out, leading to her suffering severe blood loss.

Two years on, Ms Heffer is still recovering physically and emotionally from the ordeal.

She said: 'It says so much about the anti-abortion movement and how very little it knows about the healthcare needs of those who birth humans, that they could reduce this entire, harrowing, literally bone-breaking undertaking to 'oh but you can just put it up for adoption'.

'I lost nine months of income to pregnancy, I lost the ability to leave my house, to socialise, to work, to live any semblance of a normal life.'

Ms Heffer was able to live off savings during her pregnancy and she was afforded universal healthcare that centres on birth-giver – and she still found that the process was 'littered with dangers'.

Emma Campbell, co-chair of abortion rights charity Alliance for Choice, dismissed the argument that adoption is an alternative to abortion, saying: 'It's clear to me that somebody who can say that has never had a bad pregnancy.'

She continued: 'Pregnancy is not just carrying around an object in your belly and then popping it out and nine months. Pregnancy is a real bodily change.'

Ms Campbell said that pregnancy and labour are one of the highest causes of maternal mortality across the world, while unsafe abortion comes a close second.

'By deciding on behalf of a woman or pregnant person whether or not they want to continue with the pregnancy, you're actively putting them in danger,' she said.

PhD historian Carlie Pendleton, 33, grew up in a conservative part of Virginia in the American south but moved to the UK to study for a master's degree at Oxford university.

While growing up, she was surrounded by the view that 'abortion was murder' and 'you didn't do it', but soon after moving to England, she became pregnant at the age of 27.

'I pretty much knew straight away what I wanted to do,' she told i. 'At that point, I had just moved in with my partner, I was getting ready to go into the second year of my master's

degree and I was barely managing life as it was. Then all of a sudden I found out I was pregnant.'

Ms Pendleton underwent a medical abortion at a British Pregnancy Advisory Service (BPAS) clinic. Although she was expecting judgement due to where she grew up, everyone at the clinic was 'compassionate' and 'wonderful'.

'Abortion doesn't have to be anywhere near as hard as [Supreme Court judges] currently trying to make people think,' she told i. 'It breaks my heart.'

The thought of Roe v Wade being overturned was a 'gut punch', Ms Pendleton said.

'The fact that women still have to fight just to have bodily autonomy is insane because, at the end of the day, they're not talking about protection, they're talking about control,' she added.

24 June 2022

Key Fact

- Roe v Wade was a landmark ruling made by the US Supreme Court in 1973 which protects the constitutional right to have an abortion. This ruling was controversially overturned in 2022.

Adoption

Adoption might be the choice for you if you don't want to bring up the baby yourself, and you don't want an abortion.

What is adoption?

Adoption is a way of giving the baby to new parents to bring him or her up as their own. You will continue with the pregnancy and give birth, but won't look after the baby or have any legal rights or responsibility to the child when the adoption is complete.

Adoption is a formal process organised by adoption agencies and Local Authorities, and made legal by the courts. Once an adoption is made legal the decision is final and cannot be changed.

How does adoption take place?

Although you can start preparing for adoption at any time during your pregnancy, adoption is not completed until after the baby is born. You will be asked to sign a formal document agreeing to the adoption, but you cannot be asked to do this until the baby is six weeks old. This agreement does not make the adoption final.

Usually the baby will go to foster carers for a short time while arrangements are made for him/her to move to adoptive parents. The adoptive parents then look after the baby, and apply to the court for an adoption order. Once the order is granted, the adoption is final and you are no longer the baby's legal parent.

Can I change my mind?

You can change your mind before the adoption is made legal, but it may not be easy or possible to get your baby back (depending on how far the adoption has progressed). The court will decide if you can have the baby back depending on what is best for the baby. Once the adoption is made legal, the baby will stay with the adoptive parents even if you change your mind.

What to do if you want to have the baby adopted?

Deciding to have your baby adopted may be difficult. It may help you to talk with someone who can tell you more, such as:

* A doctor or nurse at your general practice

* a hospital social worker (contact your local hospital to find out if there is a social worker attached to the maternity unit)

* an adoption social worker at your local authority's social services department or at a local voluntary adoption agency

* British Association for Adoption & Fostering – BAAF works with everyone involved with adoption and fostering across the UK.

The social worker or adoption agency supporting you will arrange for adoption counselling. This is to make sure you know exactly what the adoption involves, and to talk about all your options.

2023

What are the different types of adoption?

Choosing to adopt is not a decision to be taken lightly. The process is lengthy, and many checks are required to ensure a child will be safe and happy with you. These checks, such as investigating your childhood, medical history, criminal background checks and even contact with former partners, may feel intrusive, but they are essential.

There is so much to consider, particularly what type of adoption would work best for you.

Different types of adoption

We will look into the following types of adoption:

- Closed adoption
- Independent adoption
- Open adoption
- International adoption
- Stepparent adoption
- Adoption of a relative
- Foster-care adoption (also known as early permanence adoption)
- Single person adoption
- Same-sex couple adoption

To help you ascertain which route may be right for you.

What is closed adoption?

Closed adoption refers to having no contact with the birth parents in the run-up to and following adoption. If you are adopting through an agency, you will most likely go through a closed adoption process.

When looking into this route, consider what you will say to your child when and if they have questions about their birth parents.

What is independent adoption?

An independent, or non-agency adoption, is when you know a mother who wants to put her child up for adoption and agrees that you will be the adoptive parent. This type of adoption does not involve an agency; however, checks will still be required. The adoption process, in this instance, takes place via the courts.

What is open adoption?

Open adoption is becoming more popular and means that the birth parent/s interact with the adoptive parent/s and child. In some instances, the birth family will also have contact with the child. However, all parental decisions and rights stay with the adoptive parent/s.

In 2019, 84% of adoptions had ongoing indirect contact agreements of some sort, and 25% had direct contact, mostly with siblings of the adopted child.

What is international adoption?

Also known as intercountry adoption, this is perhaps the most difficult type of adoption. This is because you must be eligible to adopt in the UK and the country of the child.

Government funding isn't available for this particular pathway; therefore, adoption costs and additional fees (such as paperwork processing) falls to the adoptive parent/s.

What is stepparent adoption?

If you are in a relationship with a person who has parental responsibility for a child and you want to become their adoptive parent, you would go down the stepparent adoption route. For this, you must be living with your partner and their child for a minimum of six months.

This would be classified as an independent adoption; therefore, you would have to go through the County Court or the Family Proceedings Court. You also need to inform your Local Authority a minimum of three months before submitting the application.

What is adoption of a relative?

This process is similar to that of a stepparent adoption; only it's for a relative. Again, this would be an independent adoption, so you would need to inform your local trust a minimum of three months before sending an application to the court.

What is foster-care adoption?

This is technically the fastest route into adoption, as you will have gone through the fostering and adoption approval process beforehand. However, there is a chance that the fostered child will be returned to their biological parents, so you must be prepared for this.

What is single person adoption?

This is exactly what the name implies; individuals who are not married or in a relationship can go through the adoption process independently. You can choose to go through an agency and opt for an independent adoption.

What is same-sex couple adoption?

Same-sex couples have had the right to adopt since 2005. You do not need to be married or in a civil partnership to adopt; however, you need to prove that you are in an enduring relationship and live together.

The adoption process may be lengthy and confusing as you take your first steps, but it is an extremely rewarding and worthwhile avenue to pursue.

30 March 2021

What is abortion?

Abortion is when a pregnancy is ended so that it doesn't result in the birth of a child. Sometimes it is called 'termination of pregnancy'.

There are two types of abortion treatment, 'Medical' and 'Surgical' abortion:

Medical abortion using the abortion pill

Some women feel that a medical abortion is a more natural process. There are two types of medical abortion

Abortion pill (also known as early medical abortion) up to 10 weeks

* Involves taking medication to cause an early miscarriage (women experience cramping, pain and heavy bleeding).

* No surgery or anaesthetic.

Abortion pill from 10 weeks up to 24 weeks

* Involves taking medication to cause the womb to contract and push out the pregnancy.

* 2 visits to the clinic are needed.

* Sometimes an overnight stay is needed on the 2nd visit – check when you book.

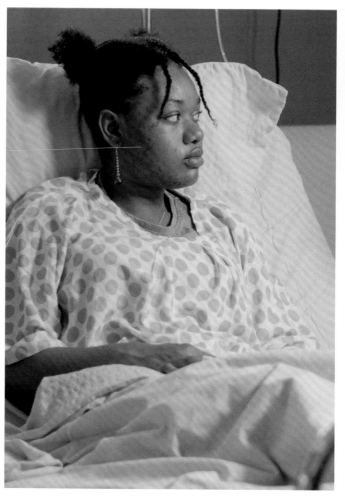

Surgical abortion

Surgical abortion involves a quick, minor operation. There are two types of surgical abortion:

Vacuum aspiration up to 15 weeks

* Removes the pregnancy by gentle suction.

* Up to 14 weeks of pregnancy this can be done with local anaesthetic. The quicker recovery time for this option means you can leave the clinic unattended and drive sooner.

* Up to 15 weeks it can be done with sedation (relaxed and sleepy).

* One visit to the clinic and you go home the same day.

Dilatation and evacuation between 15 and 24 weeks

* Carried out with general anaesthetic.

* The pregnancy is removed using narrow forceps passed through the neck of the womb and some gentle suction.

* One visit to the clinic and you go home the same day.

2023

Women's right to abortion care

Despite significant progress in recent years, too many people all over the world still face obstacles in accessing abortion care.

At MSI Reproductive Choices we are committed to every woman's right to abortion.

But what makes abortion a right worth fighting for? And what are the barriers we need to tackle to make safe abortion services a reality for everyone?

'Too many women are still denied their right to determine their own future.'

The right to safe abortion care

Abortion is a very safe and simple medical procedure to end a pregnancy. The decision to end a pregnancy is common and one that millions of people make every year. Worldwide, it is estimated that nearly one in three pregnancies ends in abortion.

Yet despite the widespread need for abortion globally, access to safe and legal abortion services is far from guaranteed to those who need them. This lack of access to abortion care is having a detrimental impact on the fundamental rights of women and pregnant people to exercise their right to make informed decisions about their health and body.

Restricting abortion only makes it less safe

While abortion care is one of the world's safest medical procedures, policy and legal restrictions continue to prevent women and pregnant people from accessing safe care.

Research shows that attempts to criminalise or restrict abortion access don't reduce the number of abortions that happen. Data from Guttmacher Institute shows that abortion rates are roughly the same in countries where abortion is broadly legally accessible and in countries where it isn't. This

is because restricting access to healthcare services does not remove the need, but forces women to seek unsafe services and add unnecessary risk to the health and lives of women.

When abortion is restricted, it is often already marginalised communities that are most at risk and disproportionately affected as they have little or no means to seek safe and legal services in another country or access private care if needed. It is estimated that virtually all (97%) unsafe abortions occur in low- and middle-income countries.

The dangers of unsafe abortion

Unsafe abortion is defined by the World Health Organization as a procedure that is carried out either by a person lacking the necessary skills or in an environment that does not meet minimal medical standards, or both.

Almost half of all abortions worldwide are unsafe, an estimated 35 million each year, as people are denied access to safe abortion care. Data shows that seven million women will face complications and over 22,000 women will die as a consequence of unsafe practices. Globally, 8-11% of maternal deaths are attributed to unsafe abortions.

'42% of women live in the 125 countries where abortion is highly restricted.'

What are the barriers to accessing abortion and how can we overcome them?

While access to abortion care has improved significantly over the past few decades, we still see unequal access between different parts of the world. Millions of women are still experiencing restrictions that limit their right to decide whether and when to get pregnant.

In every country where we work, we regularly see our services restricted by unnecessary regulation and over medicalisation. This prevents people from seeking and receiving the services they desperately want and need. Barriers to access can range from legal obstacles to stigma that leads women to prioritise secrecy over safety.

Abortion laws and legal barriers to access

Around the world, abortion laws fall along a continuum of outright prohibition to allowing abortion on request. As of 2017, 58% of women of reproductive age live in countries where abortions are broadly allowed. But while that represents the majority, 42% of women live in the 125 countries where abortion is highly restricted.

There is a long way to go until every woman's right to safe, legal abortion care is universal. But significant progress is being made every day, and we know that public support for reproductive health is growing. For example, in the UK, 9 in 10 people are pro-choice and support access to abortion care. Across the world, MSI is working with advocates to remove unnecessary policy barriers to abortion, alongside a generation of young people inspired to stand stronger than ever to protect reproductive choice.

Social barriers to access – stigma and discrimination

Even in places where abortion is broadly legal, restrictions to abortion care still exist. Stigma and other harmful social and cultural norms can inhibit both women's ability to seek services and medical professionals' willingness to provide them.

High levels of stigma are creating a culture of silence, meaning women who need safe services often lack essential information on where to access them. Stigma can stop women from speaking to their family or friends about their experience out of fear of being judged, leading to many women feeling isolated and alone throughout their experience and long thereafter. Stigma feeds silence, and silence feeds myths. Myths that misinform, mislead and further stigmatise. It's a vicious and harmful circle that we need to break.

> ### 'Stigma feeds silence, and silence feeds myths. Myths that misinform, mislead and further stigmatise.'

What MSI is doing to overcome barriers to access

As one of the world's leading providers of sexual and reproductive healthcare, we are unapologetic in our defence of a woman's right to abortion, and we are proud to provide safe abortion services wherever the law permits.

At MSI Reproductive Choices, we believe that everyone should have the right to decide their own future, on their terms.

Our work spans 37 countries providing reproductive healthcare including contraception, safe abortion and post-abortion care. We open doors. Break down stigma. And go further than anyone else to make choice possible for those who need us.

For some, choice means the ability to complete their education or start a career. For others, it means being able to look after their family. For everyone, choice means the freedom to determine their own future, creating a fairer, more equal world for all.

2023

Key Facts

- It is estimated around 97% of unsafe abortions occur in low- and middle-income countries.

- Almost half of all abortions worldwide are unsafe as people are denied access to safe care.

- Globally, 8-11% of maternal deaths are attributed to unsafe abortions.

- 42% of women of reproductive age live in the 125 countries where abortion is highly restricted.

- Abortion rates remain consistent in countries where abortion is legally permitted and those where abortion is legally restricted. What changes is that more women die of unsafe abortions in countries where abortion is hard to access.

The article on pages 9 & 10 is taken from the MSI Reproductive Choices website and printed with their permission. The copyright in this article belongs to MSI Reproductive Choices. MSI Reproductive Choices is not affiliated with and has not reviewed any other content in this publication.

The above information is reprinted with kind permission from MSI Reproductive Choices.
© MSI Reproductive Choices 2023

www.msichoices.org

Chapter 2

Laws, Myths & Facts

Does access to abortion vary across the UK?

The recent reversal of Roe v. Wade in the United States has highlighted the fragility of abortion rights. In the UK, abortion rates and access are unequal across the constituent countries, within regions and between different income groups.

By Alicja Kobayashi and Madeline Thomas

The decision by the US Supreme Court to overturn Roe v. Wade – and return decisions on whether to allow abortion to individual states – has shone a spotlight on abortion rights around the world.

While there is no imminent threat of legal restrictions on abortion in the UK, access already varies across the constituent countries. For example, despite abortion being decriminalised in Northern Ireland in October 2019 and regulations coming into effect in March 2020, access remains limited, forcing hundreds of women either to travel to other countries or to continue their pregnancy.

Abortion rates also differ within regions in the UK. They are higher for women living in deprived areas, indicating that abortion is an economic issue as well as a legal one.

What is the legal status of abortion in the UK?

Women in the UK are legally entitled to an abortion through the 1967 Abortion Act (for England, Scotland and Wales) and the Abortion (No. 2) Regulations 2020 (in Northern Ireland).

The conditions under which women can access abortion according to these two pieces of legislation are broadly similar. They include risk to the life of the mother, to the physical or mental health of the mother or any existing children in her family, or risk that if the child were to be born, they would suffer from severe physical or mental abnormalities.

In the light of the US Supreme Court decision, Labour MP Stella Creasy has warned that abortion rights in the UK are 'more fragile than people realise'. In particular, in England,

Scotland and Wales, abortions are still deemed a criminal act and doctors who do not comply with the terms of the 1967 legislation can face punishment.

As such, Creasy intends to table an amendment to the Bill of Rights to protect and enshrine women's access to abortion into law.

How accessible are abortions in the UK?

The abortion rate has increased in England, Wales and Scotland over the last 40 years (see Figure 1).

In 2021, the abortion rate for England and Wales reached its highest ever rate of 19.2 per 1,000 women residents. In Scotland, the rate has been consistently lower – at 13.4 per 1,000 in 2020 (GOV.UK, 2022; Public Health Scotland, 2021). This figure is even lower than that of the United States – 14.4 per 1,000 women in 2020 (Guttmacher Institute, 2022).

How do abortion access and abortion rates differ across the UK?

England and Wales

The number of abortions performed in England and Wales reached their highest levels in 2021. A total of 214,256 were carried out, of which 206,664 occurred in England (GOV.UK, 2022). One possible reason for the high rate is the increased availability of early abortion pills (mifepristone and misoprostol).

These were introduced in the 1990s for abortions up to ten weeks of pregnancy. They were initially both required to be taken at a clinic but from December 2018, mifepristone was

Figure 1: Abortion rate per 1,000 women residents of England and Wales and Scotland, aged 15-44

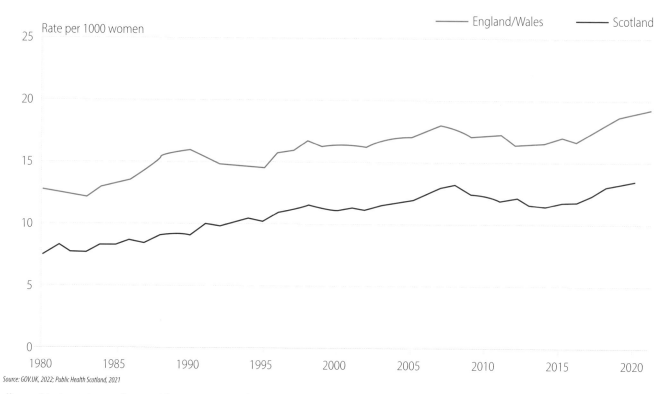

Rate per 1000 women

——— England/Wales ——— Scotland

Source: GOV.UK, 2022; Public Health Scotland, 2021

allowed to be taken at home. Then, in 2020, taking both pills at home was temporarily approved under the 1967 Act as a response to the Covid-19 pandemic (Calkin and Berny, 2021). This change has now been made permanent in England and Wales.

The overwhelming majority (around 98%) of abortions were carried out on grounds of risk of mental harm for the woman. This provision leads to what has been described as a system of de facto 'abortion on demand'.

Nevertheless, one study suggests that the requirement of two doctors' approval may cause undue stigma among abortion-seekers, and delays in rural settings where there tend to be lower availability of doctors (Calkin and Berny, 2021).

Further, research finds that women living in rural areas also face greater barriers to abortion than those in urban areas due to longer travel distances and lack of abortion services (Caird et al, 2016; Heller et al, 2016).

Longer travel distances can also impose financial barriers and necessitate unwanted disclosure of information, making it harder for women to maintain privacy. One study reports that more time away from home requires many women to turn to their family or ex-partners for childcare, which often requires an explanation (Heller et al, 2016).

Scotland

The abortion rate in Scotland is lower than in England and Wales (see Figure 1). Since 1980, the rate has risen from 7.3 to 13.5 per 1,000 women, reaching a record of 13,896 abortions in 2020 (Public Health Scotland, 2022). An additional barrier in Scotland is that abortion is not provided up to 24 weeks of pregnancy, as it is in England and Wales.

One report suggests that it is even difficult for women to access abortion services in Scotland after 18 weeks of pregnancy, although the legal maximum for England, Scotland and Wales is currently at 24 weeks under most circumstances (Sexual Health Scotland, 2021).

Apart from lack of training, it has also been suggested that a deficiency of support among medical professionals may be an important factor in explaining lower abortion accessibility in Scotland (Purcell et al, 2014). Research suggests that this may be due to negative attitudes towards late abortion among Scottish abortion providers and senior management, as well as local anti-choice views (Cochrane and Cameron, 2013).

Northern Ireland

Before March 2020, abortion access for women in Northern Ireland was severely restricted. Women in Northern Ireland were only able to access abortion services in other parts of the UK and they were not provided with funding to do so until 2017. On 31 March 2020, regulations came into effect that enabled women to access abortions legally in Northern Ireland (Armitage, 2022).

The number of Northern Irish women who obtained an abortion in England and Wales fell from 1,014 in 2019 to 371 in 2020, a drop of 641. The number of abortions accessed in Northern Ireland increased but only by 41 (from 22 in 2019 to 63 in 2020).

These numbers indicate that approximately 600 abortions that were 'expected' to occur in 2020 did not take place. One suggestion is that Northern Irish women in want of abortion services were prevented from travelling to England and Wales (largely because of Covid-19 restrictions). And further that they did not have knowledge of local services that could be accessed, resulting in these abortions not being undertaken (Armitage, 2022).

Access to abortion in Northern Ireland is still limited for many women since the relevant services have not yet been commissioned by the Department of Health and the Northern Ireland Executive. This is in spite of a deadline of the end of March 2022 that was put in place by the secretary of state in July 2021.

Regional differences

The number of non-resident abortions in England and Wales fell from roughly 32,000 in 1980 to 613 in 2021. Out of these, residents of the Republic of Ireland accounted for 33.6%, those from Northern Ireland for 26.3%, Scotland for 24.5% and the rest of the world for the remaining 15.7% (GOV.UK, 2022).

Within regions, there are also differences in the number of women accessing abortions. Those living in the most deprived areas in England are twice as likely to access an abortion compared with women living in the least deprived areas (see Figure 2). Similar patterns apply to Wales and Scotland.

This is also consistent with evidence from the United States, where studies report that nearly 50% of abortion patients live under the federal poverty line (Guttmacher Institute, 2016).

The least deprived women aged 40-44 have the lowest

Figure 2: demographic disparities in abortion rates across the UK

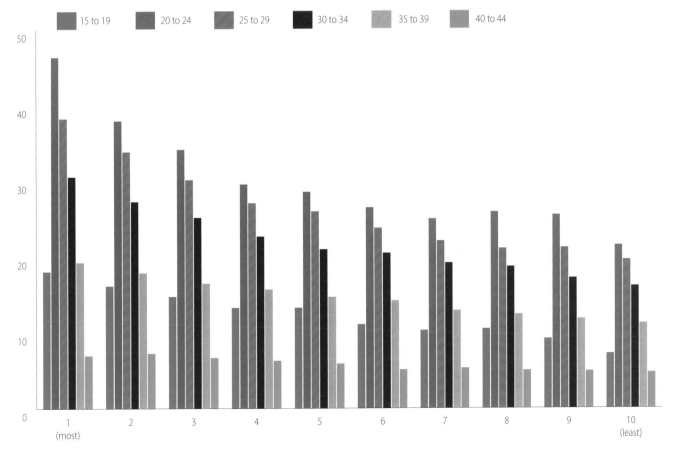

Source: GOV.UK, 2022

abortion rate at 4.7 per 1,000 women, while the most deprived women aged 20-24 have the highest at 46.4 per 1,000 women. This is almost ten times higher.

For all deprivation levels, women aged 20-24 form the largest group obtaining an abortion in England, Wales and Scotland (29% of all abortions in the UK are sought by women in this age group). The second largest group accessing abortions are women aged 25-29 (GOV.UK, 2022; Public Health Scotland, 2021).

As a result, it appears that abortion services to a great extent concern young and vulnerable women in society, for whom abortion accessibility can be highly critical in shaping their future.

Are abortion rights under threat in the UK?

There is strong support for abortion rights in the UK. A recent survey indicates that 90% of UK adults think that women should have access to abortion services (MSI Reproductive Choices UK, 2020). By contrast, in the United States 61% of adults agree that abortion should be legal in all or most circumstances (Pew Research Centre, 2022).

But there is still a worry that the reversal of Roe v. Wade will provide momentum for UK anti-choice organisations and an increase in funding coming from the United States (Oppenheim, 2022).

Jonathan Lord, medical director of MSI Reproductive Choices UK, has pointed out that UK-based anti-abortion campaigners are 'very small in number, but they are exceptionally well-organised and well-funded. The funding, which all pretty much comes from America as far as we know, will just ramp up [following the rollback of Roe v. Wade]' (Oppenheim, 2022).

A more direct threat may come from an apparent reversal of previous commitments to women's sexual health and abortion rights by the UK government in recent weeks.

As part of an intergovernmental conference on freedom of religion or belief held in London in July, the government issued a multinational statement that 22 countries signed up to. This included a pledge to repeal any laws that 'allow harmful practices, or restrict women's and girls' [...] sexual and reproductive health and rights [and] bodily autonomy'.

But the statement was later amended with references to these rights removed. The new document has been signed by only six countries, including the UK and Malta (where abortion is illegal). Human rights, pro-choice and international aid organisations have urged the immediate reversal of the amendments and a clarification of the reasons for which the deletions were made in the first instance.

This is a reminder that there needs to be appropriate government support for the supply of abortion services. This is especially the case as, despite a common legal framework, access and rates of abortion vary across the UK. Recent events in the United States show that abortion rights cannot be taken for granted.

Who are experts on this question?

- Ernestina Coast, London School of Economics
- Samantha Lattof, Maila Health
- Yana Rodgers, Rutgers University
- Brittany Moore, University of North Carolina at Chapel Hill

5 October 2022

Key Facts

- Women in the UK are legally entitled to an abortion through the 1967 Abortion Act (for England Scotland and Wales) and the Abortion (No.2) Regulations 2020 (in Northern Ireland).

- In 2021, the abortion rate for England and Wales reached its highest ever rate of 19.2 per 1,000 women residents.

Brainstorming

In small groups, discuss what you know about abortion and why it is such a controversial topic.

www.economicsobservatory.com

Abortion statistics for England and Wales: January to June 2022

Background

This report provides statistics on abortions recorded in England and Wales from January to June 2022. The data in this report should be treated as provisional and revised finalised figures will be published in the annual abortion publication.

Abortion statistics are usually published annually. Currently, the next planned date of publication will be in 2024 and will cover January to December 2022.

Commentary

Unless specified, the following commentary, charts and tables are provisional and relate only to abortions in England and Wales between January to June 2022, for residents of England and Wales.

Overall number

Between January and June 2022, there were 123,219 abortions performed on residents of England and Wales. This compares with 105,488 over the same period in 2021.

All abortions, by gestation

The total number of abortions for residents of England and Wales in January to June 2022 was 123,219. This was an increase of 17% from the same period in 2021. The majority of abortions took place in the early stages of pregnancy: 67% up to and including 7 weeks gestation; 93% up to and including 12 weeks, and 98% up to and including 17 weeks gestation.

All abortions by ethnicity

For residents of England and Wales ethnicity was recorded on 90% of the forms received for January to June 2022. Of all ethnicities recorded in the abortion statistics publication, 78% of abortions were reported as relating to women of white ethnicity, 9% as Asian or Asian British and 7% as black or black British, 5% as mixed and 1% as Chinese or other ethnic group (see Figure 3).

Statutory grounds for abortion

Under the Abortion Act 1967, a pregnancy may be lawfully terminated by a registered medical practitioner in approved

Fig. 1

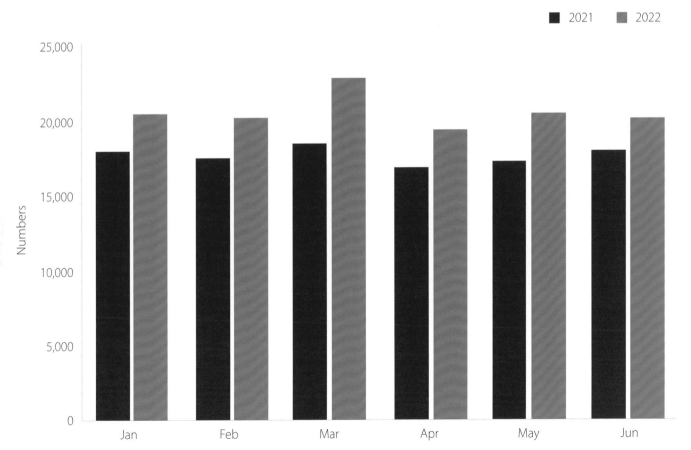

Number of abortions performed by month, resident of England and Wales, January to June 2021 and 2022

Source: GOV.UK, 2022

Fig. 2

Proportion of abortions by gestation week, England and Wales, January to June 2022

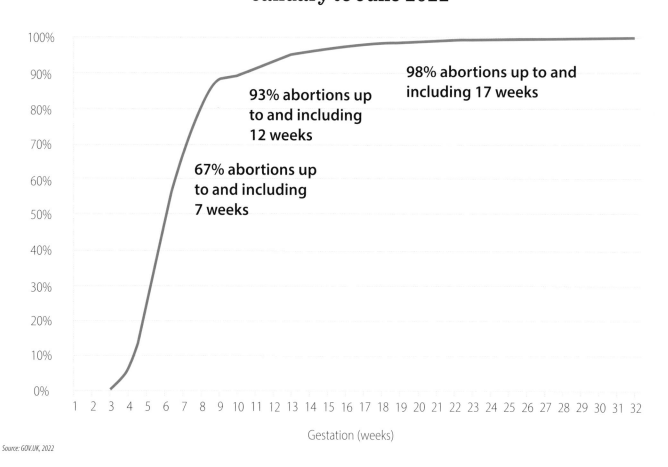

67% abortions up to and including 7 weeks

93% abortions up to and including 12 weeks

98% abortions up to and including 17 weeks

Gestation (weeks)

Source: GOV.UK, 2022

Fig. 3

Legal abortions by ethnicity, England and Wales, January to June 2022

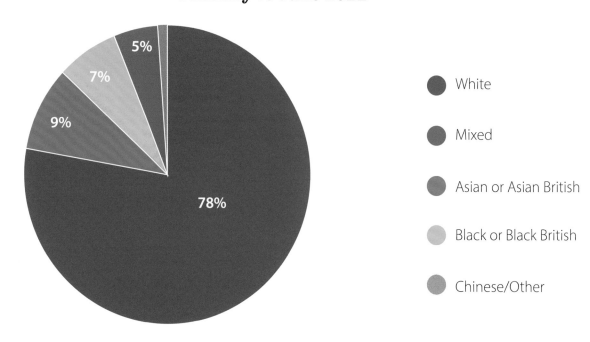

- White
- Mixed
- Asian or Asian British
- Black or Black British
- Chinese/Other

Source: GOV.UK, 2022

premises, if two medical practitioners are of the opinion, formed in good faith, that the abortion is justified under one or more of grounds A to G. (Table A). For more information about the grounds for abortion, see the Glossary and the 'Guide to abortion statistics, England and Wales: 2021' in Abortion statistics for England and Wales: 2021.

The proportion of abortions performed under different grounds has remained similar to previous years. In January to June 2022, 98.6% of abortions (121,433) were performed under ground C. A further 1.2% were carried out under ground E (1,428 abortions), with 0.2% (295 abortions) under ground D. The remaining grounds account for very few abortions; 63 in total across grounds A, B, F and G (Table 3 in 'Abortion statistics January to June 2022: data tables').

The vast majority (99.9%) of abortions carried out under ground C alone were reported as being performed because of a risk to the woman's mental health. These were classified as F99 (mental disorder, not otherwise specified) under the International Classification of Disease version 10 (ICD-10).

Table A

Grounds for abortion

Ground	Definition
Ground A	That the continuance of the pregnancy would involve risk to the life of the pregnant woman greater than if the pregnancy were terminated.
Ground B	That the termination is necessary to prevent grave permanent injury to the physical or mental health of the pregnant woman.
Ground C	That the pregnancy has not exceeded its 24th week and that the continuance of the pregnancy would involve risk, greater than if the pregnancy were terminated, of injury to the physical or mental health of the pregnant woman.
Ground D	That the pregnancy has not exceeded its 24th week and that the continuance of the pregnancy would involve risk, greater than if the pregnancy were terminated, of injury to the physical or mental health of any existing child(ren) of the family of the pregnant woman.
Ground E	That there is substantial risk that if the child were born it would suffer from such physical or mental abnormalities as to be seriously handicapped.
Ground F	To save the life of the pregnant woman.
Ground G	To prevent grave permanent injury to the physical or mental health of the pregnant woman.

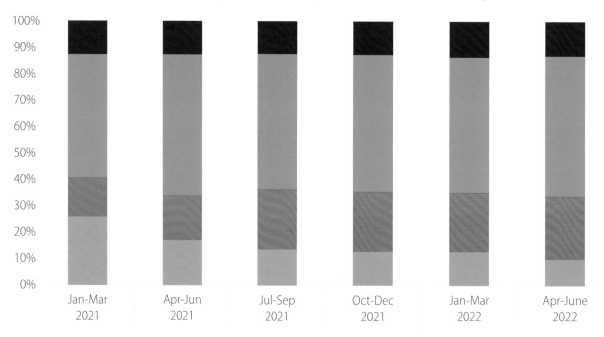

Fig. 4

Percentage of abortions performed by method, residents of England and Wales, quarterly, 2021 and January to June 2022

- ■ All surgical methods
- ▨ Both medications taken at home
- ▨ Mifepristone taken at clinic or hospital, misoprostol taken at home
- ▨ Medical abortions at hospital or clinic (inc. both medications for early medical abortion taken in clinic)

Source: GOV.UK, 2022

Method of abortion

Different methods can be used to terminate a pregnancy, depending on the gestation, and other circumstances relating to the individual woman. There are medical methods which involve the use of drugs (for example, mifepristone) and there are surgical methods, such as vacuum aspiration or dilatation and evacuation.

From January to June 2022, medical abortions accounted for 86% of abortions. This compares with 87% of abortions over the same period in 2021, and 87% of abortions over the full 2021 calendar year. The majority (97%) of medical abortions in the first 6 months of 2022 were performed at under 10 weeks, similar to the proportion in the first 6 months of 2021 (97%).

There has been a continuing upward trend in medical abortions since 1991, when mifepristone was first licensed for use in the UK. There was an additional effect during 2020 and 2021 due to the COVID-19 pandemic when the Secretary of State for Health and Social Care approved temporary measures in England to limit the transmission of COVID-19 by approving the use of both pills for early medical abortion at home, without the need to first attend a hospital or clinic. This measure was made permanent on 30 August 2022 (see press release for 'At home early medical abortions made permanent in England and Wales') and has accounted for

over 50% of terminations each quarter since April to June 2021.

Complications

Data on complications should be treated with caution. It is not possible to fully verify complications recorded on HSA4 forms and complications that occur after discharge may not always be recorded. This means that for medical terminations where either both or the second stage was administered at home, complications may be less likely to be recorded on the HSA4. The Office for Health Improvement and Disparities (OHID) is currently undertaking a project to review the system of recording abortion complications.

Complications were reported in 161 out of 123,219 cases in January to June 2022. Due to how complications are recorded, for terminations where either both or the second stage is administered at home, complications may be less likely to be recorded.

24 August 2023

Ministers urged to relax abortion laws in Great Britain after woman jailed

Labour MP criticises 'chilling' effect of legislation amid anger at sentence for termination outside time limit.

By Ben Quinn

Ministers are facing calls to 'step up' and decriminalise abortion in Great Britain after a woman was jailed for terminating her pregnancy, as an influential Labour MP said she hoped her party would act if it won power.

The call by Dame Diana Johnson, who previously tried to repeal the 1861 Offences Against the Person Act with a backbench bill, said ministers should act to change laws that were also having a 'chilling' effect on doctors, midwives and others.

Caroline Nokes, the Conservative chair of the Commons women and equalities committee, said abortion legislation was 'very out of date' and should be overhauled, after a woman was jailed for procuring drugs to induce an abortion after the legal limit.

There was outrage on Monday after the woman, a mother of three, was sentenced.

She received the medication under the 'pills by post' scheme, which was introduced during the Covid pandemic for unwanted pregnancies up to 10 weeks, after a remote consultation.

The woman, 44, pleaded guilty in March under the Offences Against the Person Act and will serve half of her 28-month sentence in custody and the remainder under licence. She had originally pleaded not guilty to a charge of an offence of child destruction.

Nokes said the judge in the case had indicated he had believed there was a clear case for parliament to reconsider legislation surrounding abortion.

'I think he has a valid point. This is not something that has been debated in any great detail for many years now,' she told Radio 4's World Tonight programme on Monday.

'And cases like this, although are tragic and thankfully very rare, throw into sharp relief that we are relying on legislation that is very out of date. It makes a case for parliament to start looking at this issue in detail.'

Speaking on Tuesday morning, Johnson said Great Britain as a whole had also fallen behind Northern Ireland, after MPs voted to liberalise abortion there, telling BBC Radio 4's Today programme: 'Society has moved on, healthcare has moved on, and I think parliament has a role now to look at reforming our abortion laws.'

There was a more cautious reaction from Lucy Powell, the shadow culture secretary, who told Sky News there was a need for 'better guidance and clearer sentencing rules'.

A former chief crown prosecutor has said he would not have prosecuted the woman at the centre of the case, saying he would have factored in the 'terrible choices' people were having to make during the pandemic.

Citing public feeling towards laws restricting abortions and her mitigating factors, Nazir Afzal told the Today programme: 'Had I been involved, had I been doing this particular case, I would not have prosecuted it.'

The number of women and girls facing police investigations and the threat of life imprisonment under abortion laws has risen over the past three years, according to the British Pregnancy Advisory Service (BPAS).

In 2022, a woman who used abortion medication in a failed attempt to end her own pregnancy was reported to the police by her medical team.

In the case of the woman jailed on Monday, prosecutors said she had knowingly misled the BPAS by saying she was below the 10-week cutoff, when she believed she was about 28 weeks pregnant.

Doctors later concluded the foetus was from 32 to 34 weeks gestation (between seven and eight months) at the time of termination. In England, Scotland and Wales, abortion is generally legal up to 24 weeks but is carried out in a hospital or clinic after 10 weeks.

Stoke-on-Trent crown court heard how the woman had discovered she was pregnant in December 2019 before arranging a telephone consultation with BPAS in May 2020.

13 June 2023

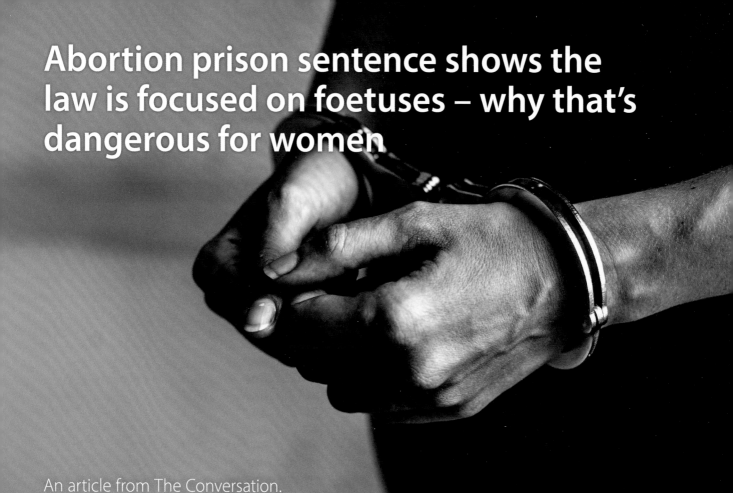

Abortion prison sentence shows the law is focused on foetuses – why that's dangerous for women

An article from The Conversation.

By Emma Milne, Associate Professor in Criminal Law and Criminal Justice, Durham University

The imprisonment of a woman in the UK for taking abortion pills at 32-34 weeks of pregnancy has shocked many. Most people are still unaware that abortion at any stage of pregnancy is illegal in England and Wales, unless authorised by two doctors.

Any woman who obtains abortion medication from sources other than an official provider faces the prospect of life imprisonment under the Offences Against the Person Act 1861. As does any woman who uses legally obtained medication in any way other than as directed, for example, delaying taking the medication.

Abortion (or 'procuring a miscarriage') was made a criminal offence to protect women from the dangers that backstreet abortion posed in the 1800s. At this time, all abortions were surgical abortions. There were no antibiotics, and few remedies if the procedure caused uncontrollable bleeding.

Today, abortion is incredibly safe when it can be legally accessed – far safer than it is for a woman to continue a pregnancy to full-term. Which leads to the question: what is the purpose of the offence today?

Reading the sentencing hearing from this and other cases, it appears the law is being used to protect foetuses.

In his sentencing remarks, the judge focused on the late stage of the woman's pregnancy. Arguing that this was an aggravating factor of the case, he describes the woman's 'daughter' as 'stillborn'.

It is important to note here that the offence of procuring a miscarriage (as detailed in the Offences Against the Person Act) makes no reference to the gestational stage of the pregnancy. The offence is also not dependent on the death of the foetus.

No woman who has illegally ended her pregnancy (for example, by obtaining abortion medication illegally) at an early gestational stage has been prosecuted. This suggests the application of the law is focused on protecting foetuses that could survive if born alive – not on preventing abortion.

Extreme vulnerability for women

This case may have further horrified many people due to the stage the woman's pregnancy had reached at the time she took the abortion medication.

The limited details of the woman's experience that are outlined in the sentencing remark indicate that she, like every other woman whose case I have examined, acted from a place of extreme vulnerability and profound crisis. The reality is that no woman wants a late-term abortion. The motivation to seek one comes from a place of desperation.

During the sentencing, the judge noted the woman's 'deep emotional attachment' to her unborn child, a common experience for women in similar situations. These are not simply 'unwanted' pregnancies resulting in delayed abortions.

Women who self-abort pregnancies late in gestation do not necessarily want the unborn baby to die. This is the situation of a woman who believes it would be impossible, possibly due to fear of violence or abuse, for her to bring a child into the world.

The role of the criminal law

Some may argue that a late-term foetus is no different to a newborn baby, and that both need criminal legal protection. But such application of the criminal law carries significant risks for women, as well as for babies and foetuses.

In the US, many states now explicitly protect the unborn child, resulting in women being arrested, detained and imprisoned following miscarriages and stillbirths, after exerting their right to refuse medical care during pregnancy, and for behaviour that would be legal if they were not pregnant.

As with almost all forms of crime control, it is the most vulnerable people – women of colour and those of lower socioeconomic status – who have been disproportionately criminalised. In addition, a direct line can be drawn between foetal protection laws and the overturning of Roe v Wade, the supreme court case that protected the right to an abortion in the US. Protecting a foetus in law is a direct threat to reproductive rights.

The criminalisation of pregnant women has also had disastrous consequences for foetuses and babies. While the aim of foetal protection laws is to prevent harm to unborn babies, the threat of legal sanctions against pregnant women has led many to actively avoid medical care during their pregnancy due to a fear that they will be reported to the police. Lack of antenatal care is a leading factor in pregnancy complications.

There is also evidence that women in the US have sought abortions to escape prosecution under foetal protection laws. For example, one woman who was charged with the reckless endangerment of her foetus after inhaling paint fumes, had the charges against her dropped after she terminated the pregnancy.

Attempts to 'protect' foetuses are, in some instances, resulting in worse health outcomes, or even death, for both foetuses and pregnant women.

Whether the criminal law should protect foetal life is a complex question, but it is a question for parliament alone. The courts and the Crown Prosecution Service, who decide to prosecute women, have interpreted procuring a miscarriage as a crime against a foetus. They have decided that women should be punished if their actions in later pregnancy cause the death of an unborn child.

Their interpretation of the law moves the statute beyond the intentions of parliament when enacted. It is time parliament involves itself in this area of criminal law, conducting a thorough and compassionate review.

16 June 2023

Key Fact

- Abortion at any stage of pregnancy is illegal in England and Wales, unless authorised by two doctors.

Discuss

In small groups, consider the effects that laws restricting abortion can have on women's health and on wider society.

THE CONVERSATION

The above information is reprinted with kind permission from The Conversation.
© 2010-2024, The Conversation Trust (UK) Limited

www.theconversation.com

The top claims about abortion, fact-checked

By Samantha Putterman

Does abortion cause infertility? Can foetuses feel pain in the first term? Is it common for women to seek abortions later in pregnancy?

Google any of these questions and you'll find a range of contradictory answers.

After nearly five decades of federally protected abortion access in the U.S., the Supreme Court's June 24, 2022, decision to strike down Roe v. Wade refuelled a host of unfounded claims.

Although views diverge on the morality of legal abortion access, research provides real data that can answer some of these questions.

Here, we compiled the most prevalent fact-checkable claims about abortion, along with a few newer claims that have surfaced since Roe was overturned.

Claim: 'Abortion is dangerous.'

Decades of research has shown that both in-clinic and medication abortions are safe for patients who seek them.

The majority of abortions are performed in outpatient, non-hospital settings, and complications are rare: About 2% of women experience a complication associated with the abortion, according to the American College of Obstetricians and Gynaecologists. When complications do occur, most are minor and easily treatable with follow-up procedures or antibiotics.

The risk that a woman will die in childbirth is significantly higher than the risk she will die from an abortion, evidence shows. Serious complications from abortions continue to be rare at all gestational ages.

'One thing people fail to understand is that pregnancy actually carries real risk, and we tend to hide all of the difficult realities about it,' said Tracy Weitz, an American University professor and senior fellow with the Women's Initiative at the Center for American Progress, a liberal-leaning think tank.

A 2004 study published in the *American Journal of Obstetrics and Gynaecology* showed that the risk of abortion complications increases as a pregnancy progresses. But researchers say that about 90% of abortions occur within the first trimester, when the procedure is safest.

Medication abortion, a two-drug combination that can be taken up to around 11 weeks into a pregnancy, is considered the most common way to terminate a pregnancy in the U.S., according to data by the Guttmacher Institute, an abortion rights research organization.

Research has shown that patients can safely self-manage their abortions using medication they access through the mail or by telemedicine. But other abortion-inducing methods that some patients turn to, such as intentionally hurting themselves or taking toxic herbs, are inherently dangerous and not recommended.

Claim: 'Abortion can cause infertility.'

Having an abortion does not typically affect a woman's ability to get pregnant again.

A 2018 report from the National Academies of Sciences, Engineering, and Medicine on the safety and quality of abortion care found no association between abortion and secondary infertility, the inability to conceive or carry a baby to term after previously giving birth. It also found no association between an abortion and subsequent pre-term birth.

Other studies have reaffirmed this and the American College of Obstetricians and Gynaecologists maintains abortion does not increase infertility risk.

One rare exception can occur in instances in which uterine scarring results from an infection following a surgical abortion procedure, known as dilation and curettage, or a D and C. This condition is known as Asherman syndrome, which can cause recurrent miscarriages or difficulties conceiving.

But this uncommon condition is not unique to people who get abortions. Patients can also undergo D and C procedures following incomplete miscarriages and in cases in which they deliver a baby but fail to deliver all or part of a placenta. The risk of developing Asherman's syndrome can also increase if someone has had an operative hysteroscopy, a history of pelvic infections or has been treated for cancer.

Claim: 'First-term foetuses can feel pain.'

When a person is injured, a signal travels through a series of nerves to the spinal cord and the brain. The information is then transmitted through a web of neurons to the cerebral cortex. It's in this part of the brain that a person perceives the feeling of pain.

The vast majority of research has found that the connections needed to transfer these signals, and the brain structures needed to process them, are undeveloped before 24 weeks of gestation, according to the American College of Obstetricians and Gynaecologists. Because a foetus at this stage of development lacks these connections and structures, reproductive experts conclude that a first-term foetus does not have the capacity to feel pain.

'Every major medical organization that has examined this issue and peer-reviewed studies on the matter have consistently reached the conclusion that abortion before this point does not result in the perception of pain in a foetus,' the organization says on its website.

Some researchers argue that pain is a subjective experience that's difficult for doctors to measure. Some researchers have suggested that providers consider anaesthetic options for the foetus during an abortion, a service that could carry additional costs.

Weitz said the argument often gets used in politics as a pretext to outlaw abortion altogether. 'What I think people need to understand is that even the scientists who are saying, "Let's debate the meaning of pain" aren't suggesting it as a justification for banning abortion,' she said.

Claim: 'Most Americans support abortion.'

Abortion is a complex topic that is difficult to poll. U.S. abortion surveys indicate that a slight majority of Americans support some form of abortion access, but not outright. Experts told us that results often vary significantly depending on how pollsters frame questions.

'There is ample evidence that many people are ambivalent about the issue or experience significant cross-pressures in formulating an opinion,' Scott Keeter, a senior survey adviser to the Pew Research Center, told PolitiFact in May. 'These realities make it quite difficult to sum up abortion attitudes in one or two sentences or with one or two questions.'

Polls taken before the Supreme Court's decision to overturn Roe v. Wade showed that a 2-1 majority of Americans didn't want justices to take that step. But other survey results show the public's views on abortion neither start nor end there.

For example, one common question asks whether abortion should be legal in all cases, legal in most cases, illegal in most cases or illegal in all cases.

If support for having abortion legal in all cases and legal in most cases is grouped together, the results in four recent surveys range from 59% to 65%. But if you group together the two middle categories – people who want to allow some abortion rights along with people who desire limited access – these results add up to 54% to 60%.

The circumstances surrounding abortions also elicit nuanced survey responses. A 2018 Gallup poll found that people widely support abortion access after rape or incest, and are more willing to support abortion in the first trimester instead of the third.

University of Notre Dame researchers conducted 217 in-depth interviews across six states in 2019, and concluded, 'Abortion attitudes are more complex than survey statistics suggest. Survey summaries can be misleading and should be interpreted with caution.'

Claim: 'Abortion causes breast cancer.'

There is no evidence that abortion causes breast cancer. Decades of research has shown no causal link between the two.

In 1997, the *New England Journal of Medicine* published a Danish study with 1.5 million participants that used information from national registries and found no link between abortion and breast cancer. The American Cancer Society calls this the largest, and likely most reliable, study on the topic.

'There is no association between a history of abortion and breast cancer. This has been clearly disproven,' said Dr. Daniel Grossman, an obstetrics, gynaecology and reproductive sciences professor at the University of California, San Francisco.

The claim of a link appears to have stemmed from hypotheses that hormonal changes caused by interrupting a pregnancy could increase a woman's susceptibility to breast cancer. Research has concluded that this isn't the case. But the premise is based on the real effects of hormones, which change throughout a woman's life – including during pregnancy – and can influence the chances of developing breast cancer later in life, according to the National Cancer Institute.

In its 2018 report, the National Academies of Sciences, Engineering, and Medicine said many older studies that

explored a possible association between breast cancer and abortion were flawed by recall bias and a lack of controls for important factors such as the woman's age.

This included one 1996 analysis that, according to the Guttmacher Institute, combined results from numerous flawed studies and concluded that abortion elevated the risk of cancer. Rather than relying on medical records, researchers asked women whether they ever had an abortion – but that methodology creates its own bias, experts say.

'Surveys have shown that 60% of people will not disclose if they've had an abortion,' Weitz said. 'When someone has a disease or chronic illness, they're more likely to recall and include all of their medical history. So, all the people who didn't have a reason to disclose that they had abortion are more likely not to tell others.'

Several other studies published since the Danish study have also concluded that induced abortion is not associated with an increase in breast cancer risk.

Claim: 'Plan B is a form of abortion.'

No. Plan B is an emergency contraceptive used to prevent pregnancy. It does not cause abortions.

Plan B, also known as the morning-after pill, is known to be effective only before a pregnancy is established, medical experts said, and can be taken within five days after sexual intercourse.

'Emergency contraception can prevent pregnancy after sexual intercourse and is ineffective after implantation,'

the American College of Obstetrics and Gynecology said. 'Studies of high-dose oral contraceptives indicate that hormonal emergency contraception confers no risk to an established pregnancy or harm to a developing embryo.'

A representative for Foundation Consumer Healthcare, the company that owns Plan B, previously told PolitiFact that the medication has 1.5 milligrams of levonorgestrel, 'the same active ingredient used in many regular oral contraceptives for over 30 years – just at a single, higher dose,' and works by temporarily delaying ovulation.

Scientific data shows that Plan B does not prevent or interfere with implantation of a fertilized egg, will not affect a woman's fertility and cannot induce an abortion, the company said.

Claim: 'More access to contraception increases abortion demand.'

Data shows this is wrong.

The U.S. Centers for Disease Control and Prevention reports that most unintended pregnancies result from women not using contraception or using it inconsistently or incorrectly. The Brookings Institution in 2012 found that unintended pregnancies account for more than 90% of abortions.

Research shows that improved contraception use has played a large role in reducing unintended pregnancies and subsequently, abortions.

One 2016 analysis by Guttmacher found that a steep drop in abortions from 2008 to 2011 was driven by a decline in unintended pregnancies spurred largely by more and better contraceptive use.

Claim: 'A "foetal heartbeat" can be detected at six weeks gestation.'

Some states have passed laws to ban abortions around six weeks of gestation, when some anti-abortion advocates say an embryo's heartbeat is detectable by an ultrasound.

Many medical and reproductive health experts, however, counter that it's medically inaccurate to describe the sounds heard over an early ultrasound as a heartbeat. Those sounds represent embryonic cardiac activity from a primitive tube of cells, experts said, but the heart is not yet formed and cannot produce an audible heartbeat.

'What is heard is the rhythmic flow of blood through the cardiac tube,' Grossman said. 'The heart isn't fully formed until nine to 10 weeks.'

Claim: 'Women routinely have late-term abortions.'

Although we have heard the phrase 'late-term abortion' often in political discourse, reproductive health experts say it's not a recognised medical term.

The American College of Obstetrics and Gynecology says the term has 'no medical significance,' and is not used in a clinical setting or to describe abortion care later in pregnancy.

'Abortion later in pregnancy is very safe and typically occurs as a result of complications in the life or pregnancy of a pregnant person,' a spokesperson for the organization said in an email to *PolitiFact*. 'Approximately 1% to 2% of abortions occur after 21 weeks, and approximately 91% of abortions occur before 13 weeks.'

A pregnancy is considered full term from 39 to 40 weeks, and late term at 41 weeks. Anti-abortion activists typically use 'late-term abortion' to describe abortions that may happen at 15 or 20 weeks, or even earlier, experts said.

Claim: 'The treatment for an ectopic pregnancy is abortion.'

Abortion-rights activists have questioned whether Roe v. Wade's overturning would limit a patient's ability to receive treatment for an ectopic pregnancy. While ectopic treatment consists of terminating the pregnancy, we found that the process is different from abortion in most cases.

Ectopic pregnancies happen when a fertilized egg implants itself outside of the uterus, usually in one of the fallopian tubes. These pregnancies are not viable and if untreated can lead to life-threatening bleeding. Most of the medical experts we talked to were clear that they don't consider ectopic treatment an abortion, but they noted that the lack of consensus over how abortion is defined makes defining ectopic pregnancy treatment confusing.

Treatments for ectopic pregnancies depend on how far along the pregnancy is. In most cases, the condition is treated as soon as possible to avoid the fallopian tube from rupturing. If detected early enough, ectopic pregnancies can be treated with a prescribed medication called methotrexate.

The drug can be used alongside another medication, misoprostol, to end viable, first-trimester pregnancies. But the price and possible side effects make it less likely to be used in abortions, Amy Addante, an OB-GYN and fellow with Physicians for Reproductive Health, told PolitiFact.

If an ectopic pregnancy is farther along, or if it leads to the fallopian tube bursting, the patient will need surgery. This can be done laparoscopically; a doctor makes a small incision and uses a thin tube with a camera and light to perform the surgery. If an emergency surgery is required, a doctor will make an incision in the patient's abdomen. Neither of these procedures are performed in a surgical abortion.

But reproductive health experts told us that the larger issue is whether medical providers interpret restrictive abortion laws as limiting their ability to treat patients with ectopic pregnancies, which comes down to how abortion is defined.

In medical terms, abortion is broadly considered a procedure undertaken to end a pregnancy. When it comes to legal definition, however, what constitutes an 'abortion' is often dictated partly by whether the patient made a conscious decision to terminate.

2 March 2023

Roe v Wade overturned: what abortion access and reproductive rights look like around the world

An article from The Conversation.

By Clare Pierson

The global landscape of reproductive rights is constantly shifting. The US Supreme Court ruling that has overturned Roe v Wade – the landmark 1973 decision that protected a woman's right to have an abortion – marks a significant regression for abortion access. But it is not the only case. While countries like the US, Poland and Russia are taking steps backward, gains are being made in places such as Ireland, Colombia and Argentina.

Abortion restrictions range from laws where abortion is permitted only to protect the pregnant person's life or health, to decriminalising abortion entirely. Often, restrictions are structured around gestational time limits, such as allowing abortion only in the first trimester.

Some laws allow for abortion on socioeconomic grounds, for example in Finland. And Britain's 1967 Abortion Act is an example of a broad interpretation of health that includes wellbeing. Doctors may take account of the pregnant woman's actual or reasonably foreseeable life circumstances when making a decision about the impact of continuing a pregnancy.

Where health is interpreted more restrictively, such as in Zimbabwe, Morocco or Peru, abortion may only be available if a pregnant person's physical health is in danger. In other regions, such as Ghana or Bolivia, language referring to mental health is explicitly included in legislation, which can widen abortion access.

In some regimes, abortion can be performed later in pregnancy based on the health of the foetus, especially in cases of serious anomaly. This is the case in Croatia. Despite this, anti-choice sentiment in the country recently led to a woman being denied an abortion after her foetus was diagnosed with a serious brain tumour. After four denials by Croatian hospitals, the woman was advised by doctors to travel to neighbouring Slovenia. But following media and public outcry, she was finally permitted to have an abortion in Croatia.

The most liberal abortion laws are those where abortion has been removed from criminal law entirely. Decriminalisation permits abortion without penalty and prioritises the safety of pregnant people in making health decisions.

Northern Ireland decriminalised abortion in 2019 following an international human rights inquiry into its abortion laws and subsequent intervention from Westminster. The Abortion (Northern Ireland) Regulations 2020 came into effect in March 2020. These regulations allow abortion up to 12 weeks on request, and after that on specific grounds of severe foetal impairment and fatal foetal abnormalities.

While Northern Ireland's abortion laws have been liberalised, this does not necessarily mean abortion is easily accessed.

The government has failed to fully commission services, meaning that abortion is being provided on an ad hoc basis by health trusts in Northern Ireland. Some women seeking abortions have continued to travel to England, illustrating how political deadlock can limit abortion access.

More restrictive

In some countries, abortion is prohibited entirely, or only to save the pregnant person's life. Malta is the only EU country where abortion is banned under all circumstances. Malta has recently seen a pro-choice movement emerge.

Draconian restrictions on abortion also affect general reproductive and maternal care, like miscarriages and ectopic pregnancies. They can delay decision making with urgent medical care when the rights of the foetus are considered equal to the rights of the pregnant woman. In El Salvador, women have been prosecuted and imprisoned for having miscarriages or attempting to procure an abortion. Charged under aggravated homicide, a sentence can be up to 50 years.

In the Republic of Ireland, before liberalisation in 2018, abortion laws affected all aspects of maternal healthcare. The foetus was viewed to have equal rights to the pregnant woman, allowing healthcare professionals to overrule her requests. In 2014, a pregnant woman who was brain dead was kept on life support for four weeks against the wishes of her family, on the basis that the right to life of the foetus could have been breached.

Activist movements to liberalise abortion laws have made significant gains in the last few years as seen on the island of Ireland, but also in Colombia where the constitutional court decriminalised abortion up to 24 weeks in 2022. In Argentina, abortion has been legal on request in the first 14 weeks of pregnancy since 2020.

Outside the law

Progress on abortion rights has been cyclical, not linear. As we are seeing in the US, anti-abortion movements continue to push back against any gains that are made. Regression on reproductive rights often correlates with wider backlashes on gender rights and the rise of far right and populist political regimes.

Laws are just one part of abortion access. Conscientious objection by healthcare professionals, regulations targeting abortion providers, stigma and protests at clinics all make it more difficult and riskier to obtain an abortion.

Even in countries with less restrictive laws, there are movements outside of legal frameworks to help people access abortions and healthcare, by assisting with travel or financial support.

While these activist networks and organisations are often viewed as sticking plasters that won't be needed when restrictions are relaxed, the reality is that barriers to abortion continue to exist after laws change. The England-based organisation Abortion Support Network continues to help around 60 women a year from Ireland, four years after abortion laws were liberalised. These efforts are just as much a part of reproductive rights as the legal framework – and their work is not finished when laws change.

24 June 2022

Down's woman vows to fight abortion law discrimination in Supreme Court

By Simon Caldwell

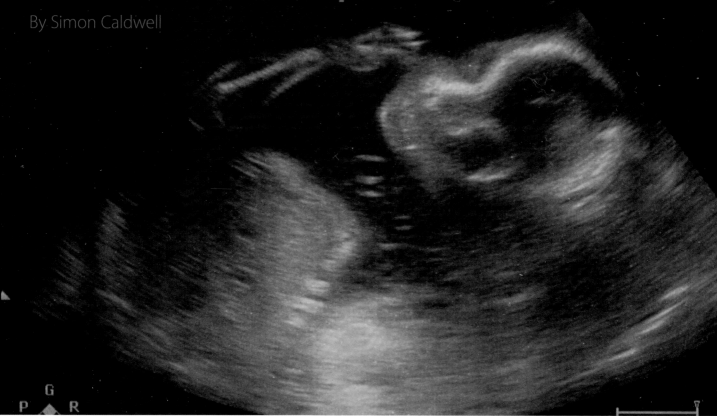

A woman with Down's syndrome is to take her fight to halt abortions up to birth for babies with her genetic condition after the Court of Appeal rejected her case.

Heidi Crowter, 27, of Coventry will apply for permission for her case to be heard at the Supreme Court following her defeat in London.

She argued that a clause in the 1967 Abortion Act discriminates against Down's syndrome children and babies with disabilities by allowing them to be killed up to birth simply because they are different from other children.

Abortion for children without Down's syndrome or other disabilities is forbidden after 24 weeks of gestation and Ms Crowter had asked for the law to apply to all unborn babies without discrimination.

Ms Crowter has claimed that the law as it is stigmatises people with Down's syndrome and disabilities by sending out the message that their lives are less valuable than those of other people.

'I feel like crying,' said Ms Crowter outside of court.

'We face discrimination every day in schools, in the workplace and thanks to this verdict the judges have upheld discrimination in the womb to which is downright discrimination,' she told journalists.

'When Wilberforce wanted to abolish the slave trade he didn't give up when things didn't go his way.

'I won't give up either because the law should be changed to get rid of a negative focus on Down's syndrome – even the words used in it are offensive.'

She added: 'This law was made in 1967 when we were not even allowed to go to school because of our extra chromosome, so I think it's time that the judges move with the times and actually meet people with Down's syndrome and see the people behind the chromosome.'

Paul Conrathe of Sinclairslaw, her solicitor, said that the judgement was 'disappointing and perplexing'.

He said: 'Rather than affirming the equal value of those with disabilities, it further adds to the stigmatisation they suffer.

'This is for the simple reason that the court concluded that the perceptions of people with disabilities about a law which allows the ending of a life because of disability are irrelevant. Yet the law protects the unborn without disabilities, leading to the understandable perception that disabled lives are of lesser value or no value at all.

'Despite this obvious discrimination the court concluded that other people – including people who are not disabled – had a different view of the implications of this legislation and the perceptions and feelings of the disabled could not be relied upon to establish an interference with their human rights.

'The conclusions of the Court are all the more surprising as Mencap, the leading UK disability charity, had informed the Court that UK abortion law conveyed "the powerful message that a life with a disability is a lesser life, even a life not worth living. It should have no place in a modern inclusive society that values all people".

'Similarly, the UN Committee on the Rights of People with Disabilities recommended that the UK change its abortion law so that it does not stigmatise those with disabilities as having a life of lesser value.'

He continued: 'By failing to give legal recognition to the suffering and stigmatisation that people with disabilities feel about a law which singles them out for termination in the womb the Court has further diminished a fragile voice for equal value.

'Yet again their perceptions are disregarded. My clients are resolute in their fight for the legal recognition of the equal value of people with disabilities and will appeal to the Supreme Court to see this anachronistic and outdated legislation changed.'

Heidi and her team have crowdfunded over £140,000 for the case.

Statistics show there were 3,370 disability-selective abortions in 2021, a nine per cent increase from 3,083 in 2020. The statistics also revealed there were 859 abortions where a baby had Down's syndrome in 2021, an increase of 24 per cent from 2020. There was a 71 per cent increase in late-term abortions at 24 weeks gestation or over where the baby had Down's syndrome, increasing from 14 in 2020 to 24 in 2021.

The actual figures may be much higher – a 2013 review showed 886 foetuses were aborted for Down's syndrome in England and Wales in 2010 but only 482 were reported in Department of Health records. The under reporting was confirmed by a 2014 Department of Health review.

The UN Committee on the Rights of Persons with Disabilities has consistently criticised countries that provide for abortion on the basis of disability.

The Committee on the Rights of Persons with Disabilities' concluding observations on the initial report of the United Kingdom of Great Britain and Northern Ireland made a key recommendation that the UK change its abortion law so that it does not single out babies with disabilities. The Government has decided to ignore this recommendation.

The Disability Rights Commission (now the Equality and Human Rights Commission) has said that this aspect of the Abortion Act 'is offensive to many people; it reinforces negative stereotypes of disability...[and] is incompatible with valuing disability and non- disability equally'.

Polling has shown that the majority of people in England, Wales and Scotland feel that disability should not be a grounds for abortion at all, with only one in three people thinking it is acceptable to ban abortion for gender or race but allow it for disability.

25 November 2022

Key Facts

- The 1967 Abortion Act allows babies with Down's Syndrome and other disabilities to be aborted up to birth. Abortion for babies without Down's syndrome or other disabilities is forbidden after 24 weeks of gestation.

- There were 3,370 disability-selective abortions in 2021, a nine per cent increase from 3,083 in 2020. The statistics also revealed there were 859 abortions where a baby had Down's syndrome in 2021, an increase of 24 per cent from 2020.

Abortion bans are not pro-life, they are anti-woman

The recent upturning of Roe v. Wade in the U.S. raises concerns for women's reproductive safety and rights, as abortion bans make the procedure illegal in more states.

The 24th of June 2022 saw the US Supreme Court make its final ruling on abortion access, with 5 of the 9 judges voting in favour of overturning Roe v. Wade, subsequently creating a complete abortion ban in seven states, and 17 other states soon to follow.

The overturning of Roe v. Wade shows not only a disregard for women's choices and human rights but also represents a wider assault on reproductive rights for all who can get pregnant.

What the overturning demonstrates is a disregard for all except those who identify as, and are biologically male.

Access to safe abortions is now at risk for millions of people in the U.S.., as abortion bans have made the procedure illegal in some states, with the overturning of Roe v. Wade – the case that established women's constitutional right to abortion in 1973.

Abortion is a medical procedure that terminates a pregnancy, which millions of women, girls and people with wombs use every year. Around 1 in 4 pregnancies end in an abortion every year, according to Amnesty International.

According to the UNFPA's *2022 State of World Population* report, almost half of all pregnancies worldwide are unintended, and over 60% of these may end in abortion. If abortion is not made a legal procedure, it will still occur – but unsafely.

While pro-life arguments insist that life begins at conception, and all pregnancies should be carried out, researchers and women alike raise concerns about the health and economic consequences this could induce. It has been pointed out that those arguing for the 'protection of life' (indicating that a baby is being killed when aborted as an embryo) are overlooking the serious consequences pregnancy can have on both a mother and their child.

Some of the frequent complications women can develop during their pregnancy include:

- Deep vein thrombosis in pregnancy
- High blood pressure (hypertension)
- Itching and intrahepatic cholestasis of pregnancy
- Anxiety and depression
- High blood pressure
- Gestational diabetes
- Infections such as UTIs
- Preeclampsia
- Preterm labour
- Miscarriages
- Stillbirth
- Severe, persistent nausea and vomiting
- Iron-deficiency anaemia
- Ectopic pregnancy
- Placental complications
- Amniotic fluid complications

- Obesity and weight gain
- Vaginal bleeding
- Convulsions/fits
- Severe vomiting

There are few other experiences which are as physically and psychologically draining as pregnancy. Pregnancy is a serious experience which can leave people disabled or mentally ill, with the process frequently resulting in injury and even death. Forcing an individual to undergo this process against their consent when safer alternatives exist can be considered barbaric and backwards.

'Pro-life' until the child is born

While consenting to sex does not equate to consenting to pregnancy, abortion exists in numerous countries as a safety net for women who are mentally, financially, or physically unready to bear a child.

The average cost of giving birth in the U.S. is between $4,000 to $15,000, and childcare costs average at $14,117 yearly. If the pro-life cause was just about protecting children, there surely must be more regulations in place for new parents to better raise, afford and protect their children.

The average cost of giving birth in the U.S.. is $4,000 to $15,000, and childcare costs average at $14,117 yearly.

Healthcare in the U.S.. is the most expensive out of every nation in the world, with some of the shortest maternity leaves and no mandatory maternal pay, concerns for the already staggering cost of food, resources, education, and overall standard of living are warranted.

Currently, around 45% of all abortions around the world are unsafe, meaning they are not done by a professional (commonly due to lack of legality), making the procedure a leading cause of maternal death on a global scale.

Banning abortion and a woman's right to choose has the potential to increase poverty in the USA, as well as create an influx of maternal health issues which most parents,

especially those below the poverty line, will be unable to pay for. As these maternal health issues increase, certain demographics will be hit harder than others with maternal mortality being two to three times higher for Black women than white women.

In cases of rape and incest, which are some of the most argued cases for advocates of abortion rights, there exists a danger of not having safe access to abortion for those who are unwillingly impregnated by an abuser.

If a girl can become pregnant after the beginning of her period, girls as young as 10 years old are at risk of becoming non-consenting mothers – posing a danger to their bodies and minds. This is a disturbing reality for young girls who are already legally allowed to be forced into child marriages in 44 U.S. states.

Girls as young as 10 years old are at risk of becoming non-consenting mothers

Along with this, babies born of incest have a higher likelihood of developing birth deformities, and children conceived through rape and abuse are at a higher chance of also being abused, too.

Abortion access isn't just about the safety and rights of women, and those who become pregnant, it is also about the safety of children potentially being born into impoverished, abusive, or unwilling families.

As the U.S. is the country with the highest amount of school shootings globally, the U.S. has done little to protect children's lives post-birth. The system does not protect children once they are born, so banning a woman's right to choose to have a child is dangerous in this regard.

Over the next few years following the overturning of Roe v. Wade the U.S. can expect to see a considerable increase in population, however, as of now both homelessness and the number of children being placed in foster care are still on the increase. Currently, 30% of all homeless people in the country consist of families with young children and there are over 400,000 children in the foster system across the country. Children in these scenarios are at increased risk of abuse, neglect and experiencing health problems – and it is apparent these numbers are only going to increase following the Supreme Court's decision. The adoption and foster care system cannot afford or manage to take in more children.

A shortage of breast milk formula occurred in the U.S. in May 2022

U.S. Republicans have traditionally held more conservative points of view regarding progressive legislation like Roe v. Wade and same-sex marriage. Whilst holding these pro-life and anti-abortion stances, numerous Republicans have continued to reject the idea of universal access to healthcare and barely vote for increasing access to the basic material needs of children with food, clothing, shelter, and childcare, and now, baby formula too. In just May of 2022, 192 Republicans voted against a $28 million aid boost for baby formula, one month before upturning Roe v. Wade.

Along with this, U.S. conservatives have frequently opposed reproductive education, including defunding and demonising Planned Parenthood – an institution which promotes healthy reproduction, sexual health information, abortion rights and more. Additionally, the constant fuelling of money between the NRA and politicians, where guns are easily, and legally accessible by young people, drives the upsurge of school shootings yearly. Politicians who vote for abortion bans do not correspondingly support the population to have more children.

As the country with the second-highest amount of unfair inequality in the world, the U.S. is currently in no state to host more children for families who cannot afford them. Combined with a lack of universal healthcare and a scarily high death rate for mothers, an abortion ban will only increase existing poverty and health crises nationally, creating a pregnancy poverty trap for women.

Controlling women with 'forced motherhood'

Having a child (with no paid maternity leave and no government payout) takes a huge toll on women's average expenses, and worsens job outcomes. Women's paychecks on average decrease after having their first child – but the drop in salary does not apply to the fathers.

What is clear is that along with stripping back the reproductive rights of those with wombs and removing the body autonomy of millions, abortion bans will increase the numbers falling into the poverty trap, disrupt education, careers, and life plans, and worsen the circumstances of women unable to leave an abusive partner. Many women die during pregnancy due to abuse and domestic homicide (particularly Black women – which is currently at one in seven).

One study highlighted how 8.4% of reported maternal mortality deaths were murders – with Black women being seven times more likely to die this way than white women. Most of these cases occurred at the hands of a domestic partner.

In the pro-life sentiment, if all life matters – why does this same sympathy not apply to a struggling mother or parent? Why has the pregnant parent's life and autonomy come second to their pregnancy?

In cases of miscarriage and sexual assault

The overturning of Roe v. Wade may also result in cases of miscarriage being called into question, mothers are at risk of being imprisoned simply for having a body which is unable to carry a child, often through no fault of their own.

In 2020, a 21-year-old Native American woman from Oklahoma was arrested for manslaughter after having a miscarriage. In October of 2021, she was convicted and sentenced to four years in prison for the first-degree manslaughter of her unborn son. Miscarriage happens in 1 in 4 pregnancies, and for many reasons – it is not a choice. Adding to this, she lost the right to vote for these four years – as voting is prohibited for many felons while incarcerated and for some time after depending on the state.

Criminalising abortion is a form of discrimination, which further fuels stigma, and will inevitably worsen the demographics of women being incarcerated. The U.S. has already got a high incarceration rate for Black and Hispanic women – and making abortion a crime will only increase this staggering incarceration rate for these communities who already struggle.

Essentially, legislation passed banning women from bodily autonomy generates a culture of women used as birthing vessels, with fewer rights than the baby they carry. As of today, there are no laws which dictate or punish men for unwanted pregnancies, even though a significant percentage of national pregnancies are due to sexual assault and the refusal to cooperate with birth control.

In some states, like Idaho and Texas, rapists' families are becoming legally allowed to sue the woman they impregnate if she chooses to have an abortion but doesn't inform the police she has been raped. If the woman fails to report the rape to the police and their physician before an abortion, a rapist's family members could sue and collect damages of $20,000 per family member, according to the bill and its legislative sponsor. This legislation demonstrates how mothers are still not in control of their bodies even when they are victims of serious harm.

Mothers are still not in control of their bodies even when they are victims of serious harm

To further display how much so this ruling is against women rather than against the death of an unborn child, we can recall that dead bodies possess more bodily autonomy rights than women. One cannot take an organ from a non-consenting person who has passed, but women will be routinely forced – and arrested if they fail – to carry out a pregnancy.

This legislation could be undoing decades of gender equality initiatives harnessed and fought for by women since gaining the right to vote.

Even with child support from a non-custodial parent, carrying, raising, and supporting a child would become a mother's main responsibility – which is undeniably difficult, in many cases dangerous, and increasingly expensive in modern-day America.

It seems the real argument in the U.S. is not surrounding whether foetuses should live, it is about whether the government can control women and people with wombs and strip constitutional rights from American citizens.

The lack of separation between Church and State in American politics and culture has undeniably stripped women of a core right with this Supreme Court ruling: the human right to choose.

6 July 2022

Global views on abortion

A majority across 29 countries believe abortion should be legal in at least most cases.

More than one in two (56%) across 29 countries believe abortion should be legal, including more than one in four (27%) who feel it should be legal in all cases.

Support for abortion is highest in Europe, with Sweden and France having the highest level of sentiment in believing abortion should be legal (87% and 82% respectively).

Support is lowest in Asia, with Indonesia and Malaysia the only countries where less than one in three think abortion should be legal (22% and 29% respectively).

Key takeaways:

- People are more likely to think abortion should be legal (56%) than illegal (28%).

- Support for abortion is highest in Sweden and France and lowest in Indonesia and Malaysia.

- People are less likely to feel abortions should be legal later in pregnancies. Sixty per cent think abortion should be legal in the first six weeks of a pregnancy while this falls to 25% after 20 weeks.

- Baby boomers are the most likely to say that abortion should be legal, while support is lowest among younger men.

How people feel about abortion

On a global level, 56% think abortion should be legal, while 28% think it should be illegal.

Looking at how this data is broken down: 27% think abortion should be legal in all cases, 29% in most cases, while 17% think it should be illegal in most cases and 11% illegal in all cases.

Support for abortion is highest in Europe. In Sweden 61% say abortion should be legal in all cases, and 26% in most cases, while only 6% and 2% think it should be illegal in most or all cases.

France is the only other country surveyed where more than one in two (56%) say abortion should be legal in all cases. A further 26% think it should be legal in most cases.

A majority thinks abortion should be legal

Thinking of abortion, which of the following is closest to your personal opinion?

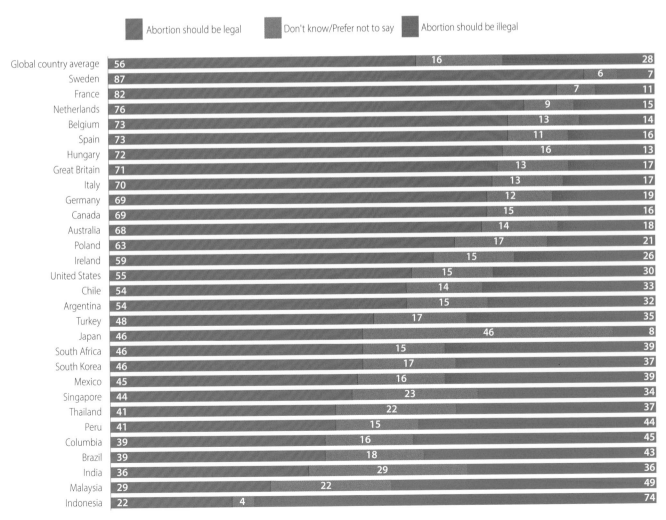

Abortion should be legal · Don't know/Prefer not to say · Abortion should be illegal

Country	Legal	DK/Prefer not	Illegal
Global country average	56	16	28
Sweden	87	6	7
France	82	7	11
Netherlands	76	9	15
Belgium	73	13	14
Spain	73	11	16
Hungary	72	16	13
Great Britain	71	13	17
Italy	70	13	17
Germany	69	12	19
Canada	69	15	16
Australia	68	14	18
Poland	63	17	21
Ireland	59	15	26
United States	55	15	30
Chile	54	14	33
Argentina	54	15	32
Turkey	48	17	35
Japan	46	46	8
South Africa	46	15	39
South Korea	46	17	37
Mexico	45	16	39
Singapore	44	23	34
Thailand	41	22	37
Peru	41	15	44
Columbia	39	16	45
Brazil	39	18	43
India	36	29	36
Malaysia	29	22	49
Indonesia	22	4	74

Source: Global Advisor • Base: 23,348 online adults across 29 countries

Opposition to abortion

Only five out of the 29 countries surveyed – Indonesia, Malaysia, Colombia, Brazil and Peru - have more people saying they are against making the option to terminate a pregnancy legal than are for it.

By some distance Indonesia is the country most against abortion. Three in four (74%) think abortion should be illegal: 37% say it should be illegal in all cases and 37% in most cases. Only 22% think abortion should be legal and of that only 1% say it should be legal in all cases.

It is the only nation surveyed where there is a difference of more than 50% between those against compared and those for. Termination of a pregnancy in the country is only legal as a result of rape or in cases of risk to a woman's health.

Three of the six LATAM countries surveyed have more against than for abortion. In Colombia 39% feel it should be legal and 45% illegal, in Brazil 39% to 43%, and Peru 41% to 44%.

The Generational and Gender divide

On a global level a higher proportion of women think abortion should be legal compared to men (59% to 52%), with 30% of women thinking it should be legal in all cases while 23% of men feel this should be the case.

A third of men (33%) think abortion should be illegal (20% in most cases, 13% in all cases) compared to 25% of women (15% in most cases, 13% in all cases).

Looking at support for abortion through a generational lens, it is younger men who have the lowest support for the issue. Less than half of Millennials and Gen Z males say they think abortion should be legal (48% and 47%). Conversely 57% of

Millennial women and 61% of Gen Z women and believe it should be legal.

Baby boomers, considered by many as the most 'conservative' generation, are the most in favour. While there is a gap in support between Gen Z women and men, this isn't the case for baby boomers. Sixty-three per cent of female baby boomers say they think abortion should be legal, while 61% of male baby boomers say the same.

When should abortion be legal?

In terms of when an abortion should be legal, if a woman's life or health is at risk has the highest support. Globally almost eight in ten (78%) say it should be legal in this instance, compared to 10% who say it shouldn't. Support is highest in Sweden (92%) and France (90%) and lowest in India (52%).

In the instance of rape, 72% globally think abortion should be legal. Support is again highest in France and Sweden (both 89%). Support is lowest in Indonesia, and it is the only country where more people say abortion should not be legal in the instance of rape compared to those that say it should be (50% to 32%). Indonesia also has the lowest support for whether abortion should be legal if the baby will be born

Male Gen Z are the least supportive of abortion

Thinking of abortion, do you agree with the following statement:
Abortion should be legal?

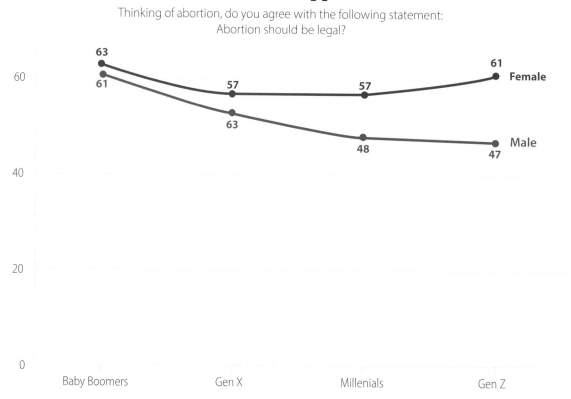

Source: Global Advisor • Base: 23,348 online adults across 29 countries

Italians differ from the rest of Europe on who should be penalised

If an abortion was carried out in a situation where it is illegal, do you think each of the following should face a penalty? (% saying 'Yes')

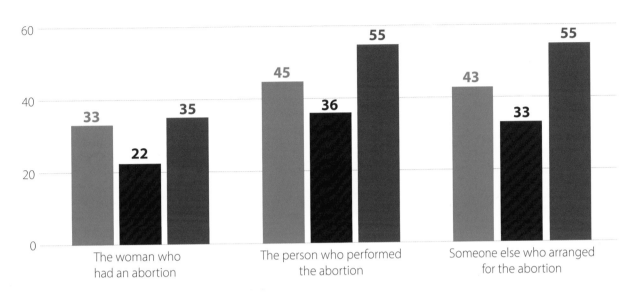

- Global country average
- Europe
- Italy

	The woman who had an abortion	The person who performed the abortion	Someone else who arranged for the abortion
Global country average	33	45	43
Europe	22	36	33
Italy	35	55	55

Source: Global Advisor • Base: 23,348 online adults across 29 countries

with severe disabilities or health problems. Only 41% say they support abortion in this instance, while 41% say they would not support a woman having an abortion.

Globally there is less support for when a baby will be born with health problems, with 65% saying they support this. France and Hungary are most in favour (84% and 82%), while in Sweden, the most consistently supportive country in this report, 75% feel abortion should be allowed.

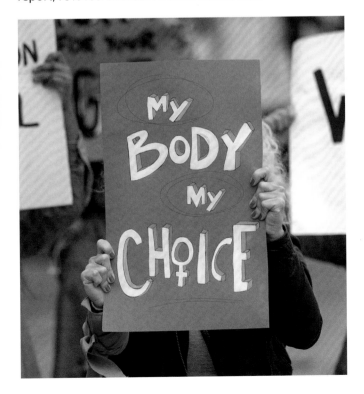

Should illegal abortions be penalised?

Looking at who is responsible in the event of an illegal abortion, people are more likely to feel the woman who had the abortion should not face a penalty. Almost one in two (47%) globally say she should not be penalised compared to a third (33%) that say she should.

People are more likely to feel those who either performed, or were involved in arranging the illegal abortion, should be punished. Forty-five per cent say the person who performed the abortion should face a penalty while 43% say the person who arranged the abortion should be punished.

However, in both cases there is a sizeable proportion of people who think neither should be penalised, with 36% feeling the person who performed the abortion shouldn't be punished and 35% say the person who arranged it shouldn't be punished.

People in North America and Europe are more likely to feel this way with the exception of Italy. While Italians are more likely to say a woman shouldn't be punished for having an illegal abortion, more than one in two feel the person who arranged the abortion and the person who performed the procedure should be punished.

22 August 2023

A year ago Roe v Wade was overturned. Grieve for the new America

The supreme court's decision has created a two-tiered class of US citizenship: one for men and one for women. It is a generational tragedy.

By Moira Donegan

That it has only been a year since the US supreme court overturned Roe v Wade and ended the federal right to an abortion feels absurd, almost impossible. How horribly and dramatically our country has changed since then. In a span of just 12 months, thousands of lives have been permanently changed – dreams dashed, intentions scuttled, childhoods abruptly ended, talents and potential suppressed, health risked, and the self- determination of pregnant women snatched from them by a body of unelected jurists who believe that their own sentiments are more important than those women's dignity.

The decision unleashed atrocities and morbid perversions of medical ethics that have rapidly become routine. Women experiencing miscarriages now wait around in emergency rooms and parking lots, unable to receive treatment until they sicken to the point where sufficiently brutal health outcomes (life-ending or life-altering, depending on the state) become a certainty. Other women, and no small number of girls, now gestate and give birth to infants conceived by their rapists – their coaches, abusive boyfriends, acquaintances, priests, fathers. Still others are forced into torturously monstrous exercises in medical futility, their bodies commandeered and used by the state to birth babies without lungs or heads.

Any one of these scenarios is the stuff of a horror movie, episodes of legally mandated medical sadism that makes a mockery of the principles of liberty, equality, privacy or due process. But the anti-choice movement also seems to be determined to bring an end to free speech: when an Indiana doctor, Caitlin Bernard, spoke to the media about performing an abortion on a raped 10-year-old girl who had had to flee Ohio for the procedure, Indiana state Republicans set about a year-long campaign of harassment and intimidation meant to punish her for speaking publicly about the reality that their policies had created.

All of this was predictable. All of it was, in fact, predicted by the pro-choice movement, whose size, institutional knowledge and internal variance did not earn it respect from either the Democratic establishment or the movement left. And it was all predicted, too, by the anti-choice movement, one of the largest and best-funded hate campaigns in the nation's history, whose habitual bad faith and single-minded commitment to ensuring women's suffering ushered in the human rights catastrophe of the post-Dobbs era entirely on purpose.

The Dobbs decision itself was not a surprise. Republicans held a commanding six-three supermajority on the court,

ever since the appointment of the arch-conservative and devout Catholic justice Amy Coney Barrett, and the plaintiffs in Dobbs, the case that provided the court the excuse to end Roe, had revised their filings to ask for a more extreme ruling as soon as she was confirmed. Activists in the anti-choice movement, and the Republicans who do their bidding, dispensed with pretense and began introducing the bills they really wanted. Laws that criminalised women for seeking abortions were introduced; laws eliminating the fig-leaf 'rape, incest and life of the mother' exemptions that the anti-choice set had long hid behind passed, and are now standard.

None of the ensuing atrocities should have come as a surprise to anyone with an interest in women's rights, because they were not a surprise: they were the anti-choice movement's design. Even the opinion itself leaked ahead of time, with a draft of Samuel Alito's rambling, contemptuous and ahistorical opinion published in Politico a month before the formal ruling.

Still, the Biden administration was inexplicably and unforgivably flat-footed in the response, seemingly caught off-guard by an outcome that they had been warned about more than a month in advance. Members of the administration seemed, if anything, a bit irritated by the demand for action, and it emerged just days after the Dobbs decision went into effect that the Biden administration was in fact planning to appoint Chad Meredith, an anti-choice lawyer, to a lifetime appointment on the federal bench. The nomination was only dropped after an outcry from an irate nation.

For months, it seemed a victory when the clearly indifferent Biden so much as said the word abortion. When the decision came down, the Biden administration had no interest in using executive power to help women exercise their rights, and no plan to restore access, to redignify American women, or to mitigate the unspeakable harm that was coming. They still don't.

For months, abortion flickered in and out of legality in many states, like a fluorescent light with a moth caught in it, as lawsuits ascended through the courts and judicial stays either permitted or prohibited women from exercising authority over their own lives. But in the 13 states with so-called trigger laws – enacted by anti-choice Republicans in drooling anticipation of the day the court overturned Roe – the Dobbs decision meant that abortion was banned immediately. In these states, abortion providers rushed to

perform as many procedures as they could before the bans went into effect, while women wept on the phone lines and in the waiting rooms, like passengers awaiting the last plane out of a war-torn country.

This was the stuff of another horror movie: the dwindling hours, the ticking minutes, that separated these women from a world where they were full citizens, endowed with the dignity to determine their own family futures and sexual lives, and one where they were transformed in law into something else, something lesser. Now, a new and chaotic legal regime has emerged, where women are full citizens in some states, something more like children in others. It is not a situation that will hold. The anti-abortion movement, and the Republicans who serve it, has every intention of pursuing a national ban, and all the resources needed to achieve it in our lifetimes.

Amid all the brutality, all the horrific medical emergencies, all the women sickening to the brink of death, all the girls forced to remain pregnant with the children of their rapists while still children themselves, there is one central feature of Dobbs and its aftermath that hangs over every crude discussion of gestational limits and unspeakably vulgar argument over rape exemptions, this is the elephant in the room: that history does move backwards, that America does not advance all of its peoples steadily toward inclusion and justice, and that Dobbs diminished the citizenship of half of America because of their sex. It came as women attained new heights of education and achievement – it aims to reverse them. It came as trans people achieved new levels of visibility and acceptance as their true selves – it aimed to shove them back into a social role determined by their sex assigned at birth.

Dobbs created a two-tiered class of American citizenship: one for those who are trusted to plan their families and control their bodies, because they are male, and one for those who are not, because they are female. It is a generational tragedy.

This is not the kind of thing we are accustomed to memorializing in America: the lost dreams, the ruined health, the unwritten novels and symphonies, the early deaths, the searing and profound humiliation. We do not like to dwell on our failures, our violences, our ignoble reversals. But it is worth dwelling on this one today. Take a moment to remember the women who have been denied abortions since Dobbs – those who are hurt and threatened by their pregnancies, and those who simply do not want them – and grieve for them. Grieve, and wonder about what other lives they might have led, if they had a choice.

23 June 2023

Research

Using this book and conducting some further research online, in small groups, answer the following questions:

- What are some of the reasons a woman might decide to have an abortion?

- Why do some people oppose a woman's right to have an abortion?

- What is the current UK legislation on abortion?

- When was Roe v Wade overturned?

The worth of disabled lives is weighed in the womb

Sir Brian Souter's comments about disability abortion are tragic but true.

By Lynn Murray

We are all used to hearing passionate views about abortion, but it seems a few eyebrows have been raised recently when hearing about a high-profile, multimillionaire transport tycoon's comments on abortions where a baby has a disability.

Sir Brian Souter, co-founder of Stagecoach, was delivering a guest sermon at the evangelical Destiny Church in Glasgow when he compared late-term abortions on the basis of disability to the infamous biblical tyrant who ordered the killing of all male babies aged two or under in Bethlehem shortly after the birth of Jesus Christ.

Souter's key point was that abortions of unborn children with minor disabilities, including conditions such as a cleft lip, are currently legal right up to birth and that is profoundly wrong in 21st century Britain.

Is the comparison somewhat hyperbolic? Yes, but does it correspond to reality?

The abortion provider, British Pregnancy Advisory Service (BPAS), confidently declares in an article by The Times that 'Mr Souter's statement that at 39 weeks gestation, a woman could legally end a pregnancy due to a hare lip is simply untrue'. But is it?

Statistics released by the Department of Health and Social Care state explicitly that 40 abortions took place in 2021 where a baby had a cleft lip or cleft palate, including six that were at 24 weeks or beyond.

It is not recorded at what gestation these six abortions occurred, but under our current law, because the 24-week time limit does not apply if the baby is diagnosed with a disability, these abortions could have legally taken place right up to the moment of birth.

The real figures could be much higher. European researchers, Eurocat, found in a 2013 review that 157 babies with either a cleft lip or cleft palate were aborted in England and Wales between 2006-2010, despite the Department of Health and Social Care recording only 14.

The fact is that aborting unborn babies due to a disability is happening more and more. In 2021, 274 disability-selective abortions were performed at 24 weeks and over, a nearly 20 per cent increase from the previous year. This points to a worrying trend of what appears to be increasing pressure on parents to proceed with abortions when their baby is found to have a disability.

Emma Mellor said she and her husband felt under continuous pressure to have an abortion from her 20-week scan – when doctors told Emma that her baby had some fluid on her brain and would likely be disabled – all the way through to when the 'baby had started travelling down the birth canal'. Emma said, 'In all honesty we were offered 15 terminations, even though we made it really clear that it wasn't an option for us, but they really seemed to push and really seemed to want us to terminate.'

At 32 weeks, a test showed that her daughter had Down's syndrome, and Emma was reminded by doctors several times that her daughter could be legally aborted until birth.

'At 38 weeks, the doctors made it really, really, really clear that if I changed my mind on the morning of the induction to let them know, because it wasn't too late.'

Make no mistake, Emma's experience is not an unfortunate one-off. Research from three Down's syndrome organisations shows that of those women pregnant with a baby with Down's syndrome, 46 per cent were offered an abortion again after informing medical professionals that they wanted to keep their baby.

As time goes on, it seems that the pressure on women to terminate their pregnancies for babies with disabilities increases. Society constantly tells us how challenging it would be financially and practically to provide the care our children deserve.

'90 per cent of babies found to have Down's syndrome before birth in the UK are aborted.'

I know this first hand. As a mother of a daughter with Down's syndrome, it horrifies me that in the UK 90 per cent of babies found to have Down's syndrome before birth are aborted (yes – you read that correctly). Not only does this practice appear to disregard the reality that many people with Down's syndrome go on to lead happy and fulfilling lives, contributing hugely to those around them, but research suggests that life expectancy for people with Down's Syndrome is nearly 60 years old now, with many living into their 70s. It is no longer around 25, as it was forty years ago due to medical neglect and institutionalisation.

In a society that attempts to pride itself on equality and inclusivity for people with disabilities, this should not be an issue that is only preached from the pulpit of Destiny Church in Glasgow, but one that unites people from across the political and religious spectrum. There is little less inclusive than perpetuating a form of ableism by singling out babies with disabilities for abortion.

Polling from Savanta ComRes in 2017 shows that only one in three of the public think it is acceptable to ban abortion for gender or race but allow it for disability. The public is right to recognise the logical implication of our current discriminatory abortion laws for babies with disabilities, which is that people with disabilities are somehow inferior or less worthy of life because of the care that they might need, an idea that is both untrue and deeply damaging.

As a transport businessman, Sir Brian Souter may be a rather unexpected voice in this debate but we would do well to heed his warning: namely that failing to support and give hope to women and families who find themselves in these situations will lead to increasingly dire consequences for how we treat these vulnerable unborn children and the ripple effect that has on our societal culture. This needs to stop.

21 March 2023

Angela Tilby: Pro-choice and -life both fall short

By Angela Tilby

OVER many years, I have listened, as a colleague and friend and also as a priest, to individual women who have wanted to talk about abortion. Those who have chosen to have the procedure to end an unwanted pregnancy often express relief, sometimes overladen with guilt; others express lasting regret. It is hardly surprising that, after the US Supreme Court's ruling to end the constitutional right to abortion, feelings in the States are running high. Donald Trump is claiming that God made the decision, and pro-choice supporters describe it as part of a fascist takeover.

Three years ago, the celebrated American priest and author Fleming Rutledge explored her own mixed responses to the issue in a helpful (if inconclusive) blog (available to read at generousorthodoxy.org).

She starts from the conviction that abortion is a violation of human life and an offence to the Creator. Yet she wonders why so many of those who are vehemently pro-life are relatively indifferent to other such violations, such as the murders committed by easily available guns. And she worries that few pro-lifers show much interest in support for those pregnant women whom they would compel to go to full term, let alone for their babies. There is a chronic shortage of babies in the Western world available for adoption; so she implies that the pro-life position falls short ethically because it fails to follow through.

Yet she cannot accept the slogan 'A woman's right to choose.' As she notes, 'There are two other human beings in this equation, the father and the unborn (not to mention God).' Pro-choice arguments simply exclude them, and that is unjust.

She compares the well-worked Roman Catholic arguments against abortion to the theological and ethical emptiness of most of the Protestant Churches, which, she says, have tended to line up uncritically with secular, pro-choice voices. (Apparently, however, since the Supreme Court's judgment, a group of Episcopalians have produced a template for a liturgy of lament and healing, which, they hope, can be used by both sides.)

She admires Mario Cuomo, who, as Governor of New York, made a speech in 1984 in which he declared his unwavering loyalty to the teaching of the RC Church at the same time as refusing to make abortion illegal.

The Church of England's stance is fairly conservative, and I am grateful for that. I am also grateful that our pastoral tradition allows us to respond to those considering or coming to terms with abortion without judgement. No individual should have to bear sole responsibility for a choice that society has shown that it cannot deal with. What I most appreciated about Fleming Rutledge's blog was her willingness to live with the discomfort of the question: she was not seeking a comforting via media between two views, but enduring, and witnessing to, the sharpness of their opposition.

24 June 2022

I kept my baby because of 'pro-lifers' and raised it in poverty. Then they called me selfish

While motherhood gave me several precious, lovely, and powerful moments, it also cost me so much.

By Jennifer Stavros

A few years ago, I found out something common to many people with wombs: I was expecting. What exactly I was 'expecting', however, was open for debate. My conservative mother was sure it was a 'blessing'. I wasn't so sure. For one thing, I was poor – really poor. I was told that if I aborted my baby, I'd be selfish. But as a poor woman, I was also told it would be selfish to raise a child in poverty. It was even suggested to me that, considering my financial circumstances, it would be selfish for me not to put my child up for adoption.

I did give birth to my children, and I don't regret it – I love them more than anything in the world. But I was pushed down the path of motherhood by Christian conservatives who described themselves as 'pro-life'. Pro-life meant convincing me to continue my pregnancy. It did not, as I soon found out, mean supporting me to raise my child when I lived in poverty.

Being a poor parent meant standing in lines for hours in cold and crowded rooms, waiting for services which would fail to be supportive. It meant sitting in welfare offices for hours, waiting to be called on, to try to get assistance for welfare benefits that weren't enough for our basic costs of living. It meant poring through pages of paperwork and sitting for hours at outdated computers in public libraries or state offices hoping to find subsidized childcare assistance, only be left disappointed as only a fraction of folks in need qualify and, even when you do, those programs have months-long waiting lists.

Have trouble affording the cost of living as a single parent? Too bad. When I was made homeless, shelters didn't know how to accommodate me as a parent. As a single mother without any drug or alcohol issues or major mental health concerns, I fell through the cracks of all the usual systems that were mostly set up to help addicts or the severely ill (laudable programs, but none that provided for me). When I did find some housing assistance, it was dependent on me working certain kinds of jobs with hours that weren't compatible with parenting. And of course, I was still on the waiting list for childcare, so I couldn't rely on that. I could have taken a different job – but then I would have lost my housing. The bureaucracy was impossible to navigate.

Being poor with housing worries means if you're lucky enough to find a short window to even apply to wait numerous years for the chance to get a Section 8 housing voucher, you may not even be able to redeem it because many modern landlords don't even take them. I placed myself on one of those lists in 2015 during a two-day opening for a waiting list. I still haven't heard back. Being a poor parent means our only existence is to work tirelessly, jumping through hoop after hoop with no guarantee that any of it will go anywhere. All the while, we are repeatedly called selfish and unfit to parent by the same people who wanted us to have babies when we were pregnant. Both family courts and dependency courts operate in ways that are stacked against impoverished parents. Your struggles will be used against you at every single turn.

While motherhood gave me several precious, lovely, and powerful moments, it also cost me so much. Though there has been joy, there has also been unbearable pain, unnecessary suffering, harsh judgements, and repeated dehumanization. The systems in place did not want me to be a parent even though they insisted that they wanted me to be a parent. They wanted my body to be a vessel for other people to be parents who better fit society's desired mould: wealthy and with two people present. I fear that that's what the Supreme Court judges overturning Roe v Wade also imagine – not that people like me will be able to successfully parent and be lived out of poverty when they continue their pregnancies, but that we will supply infants to others who want to adopt and are tired of being on a waiting list. I wouldn't wish the plight of being a poor parent on anyone. Enduring motherhood in this country, under these systems, has been almost unbearable. It simply never stops.

I yearn for a world where families are truly supported to raise their children if they choose to continue their pregnancies. I yearn for a country that looks at a scared mother who is unexpectedly pregnant but wants to parent and sees a vulnerable person to support, rather than a target for insults or someone else's opportunity. The overturning of Roe means thousands of more women living lives like mine. It was hard for me even after I made the choice to have my children. I can't imagine what it would be like to live this kind of a life after being denied access to an abortion.

24 June 2022

Further Reading

Pages 1-3: 'You can view the original article from Brook at https://www.brook.org.uk/your-life/making-a-decision-about-a-pregnancy/

Page 13: Where can I find out more?

Roe v Wade: UK anti-abortion activists use US reversal to build support: Article from Maya Oppenheim.

Abortion statistics in England and Wales: Department for Health and Social Care. Termination of pregnancy statistics: Public Health Scotland.

Abortion in Northern Ireland: decriminalisation, Covid-19 and recent data: Paper in The Lancet.

Stella Creasy moves to make abortion a human right in British Bill of Rights: Article in The Independent.

Pages 23-26
Sources:

American College of Obstetricians and Gynecologists, Combating Abortion Myths: The Tool Kit, Accessed Feb. 11, 2023

National Library of Medicine, Incidence of emergency department visits and complications after abortion, Jan. 2015

National Library of Medicine, The comparative safety of legal induced abortion and childbirth in the United States, Feb. 2012

National Library of Medicine, Risk factors for legal induced abortion-related mortality in the United States, April 2004

Guttmacher Institute, Abortion and Mental Health: Myths and Realities, August 2006 Guttmacher Institute, Medication Abortion, Feb. 1, 2021

Action Canada for Sexual Health & Rights, Abortion myths and facts, Accessed Feb. 11, 2023

Planned Parenthood, Facts about Abortion Care, July 27, 2020

Annals of Internal Medicine Journal, Health of Women Who Did and Did Not Terminate Pregnancy After Seeking Abortion Services, Aug. 20, 2019

Journal of Medical Ethics, Reconsidering fetal pain, 2020

Live Science, Do Fetuses Feel Pain? What the Science Says, Aug. 3, 2022

National Academies of Sciences, Engineering, and Medicine, The Safety and Quality of Abortion Care in the United States, 2018

The New England Journal of Medicine, Induced Abortion and the Risk of Breast Cancer, Jan. 9, 1997

Cancer.org, Abortion and Breast Cancer Risk, June 19, 2014

American College of Obstetricians and Gynecologists, Facts Are Important: Identifying and Combating Abortion Myths and Misinformation, Accessed Feb. 17, 2023

American College of Obstetricians and Gynecologists, Facts Are Important: Gestational Development and Capacity for Pain, Accessed Feb. 17, 2023

New York Times, Abortion Opponents Hear a 'Heartbeat.' Most Experts Hear Something Else, Feb. 14, 2022

Healthline, Can Abortion Cause Infertility?, Updated Jan. 16, 2020

Cleveland Clinic, Asherman's Syndrome, Accessed Feb. 26, 2023

PolitiFact, Fact-checking the false claim that Plan B causes abortions, June 30, 2022

American College of Obstetricians and Gynecologists, Emergency Contraception, Sept. 2015

PolitiFact, More access to contraception increases abortion demand? No, that's not right, Jan. 18, 2023

PolitiFact, Why polling about abortion hides the true complexity of what Americans think, May 5, 2022

PolitiFact, What do Americans think about abortion policy? It can be complicated, June 24, 2022

Gallup, Abortion poll, Accessed Feb. 27, 2023

University of Notre Dame, How Americans Understand Abortion, 2020

PolitiFact, How treatment of ectopic pregnancy fits into post-Roe medical care, June 30, 2022

Mayo Clinic, Ectopic pregnancy, March 12, 2022

Email interview, Rachel Kingery spokesperson at the American College of Obstetricians and Gynecologists, Feb. 15-16, 2023

Phone interview, Tracy Weitz, professor at American University and senior fellow with the Women's Initiative at American Progress, Feb. 17, 2023

Email interview, Dr. Daniel Grossman, professor of obstetrics, gynecology and reproductive sciences at the University of California, San Francisco, Feb. 19-20, 2023

Pages 31-33
Sources:

https://www.theguardian.com/commentisfree/2021/dec/10/arguments-abortion-us- controlling-women-anti-abortionists-women-rights-over-bodies

https://news.un.org/en/story/2022/06/1121312

https://www.washingtonpost.com/outlook/2022/06/26/abortion-birth-control-restrictions- curtail-womens-citizenship/

https://www.aclu.org/news/reproductive-freedom/what-comes-next-abortion-rights- supreme-court

https://www.nichd.nih.gov/health/topics/pregnancy/conditioninfo/complications   https://www.nhs.uk/pregnancy/related-conditions/complications/

https://www.cdc.gov/reproductivehealth/maternalinfanthealth/pregnancy-complications.html

https://www.bbc.co.uk/news/world-us-canada-59214544

https://www.theguardian.com/us-news/2020/jan/27/maternity-leave-us-policy-worst- worlds-richest-countries

https://womensenews.org/2021/10/child-brides-closer-than-you-think/ https://www.bbc.co.uk/news/world-us-canada-59214544   https://www.winniepalmerhospital.com/content-hub/pregnancy-loss-1-in-4   Contributor Profile

Useful Websites

www.asn.org.uk

www.bpas.org

www.brook.org.uk

www.carecheck.co.uk

www.catholicherald.co.uk

www.churchtimes.co.uk

www.economicsobservatory.com

www.gov.uk

www.independent.co.uk

www.inews.co.uk

www.ipsos.com

www.msichoices.org

www.nupas.co.uk

www.openaccessgovernment.org

www.politifact.com

www.theconversation.com

www.thecritic.co.uk

www.theguardian.com

Where can I find help?

Below are some telephone numbers, email addresses and websites of agencies or charities that can offer support or advice if you, or someone you know, needs it.

- **British Pregnancy Advisory Service (BPAS).**
- **Brook Young People's Information Service.**
- **Marie Stopes International.**
- **Abortion Support Network.**

More sources of information:

Social Services - contact your local social services to discuss how you can arrange for adoption.

Citizens Advice Bureau

British Association for Adoption & Fostering – BAAF works with everyone involved with adoption and fostering across the UK.

Telephone: 020 7520 0300

If you would like more help or advice about abortion you can:

- Visit a Brook service for advice and support
- Visit the British Pregnancy Advisory Service (BPAS) website, or call them on 03457 30 40 30 from the UK or on +44 1789 508 211 from elsewhere
- Visit the National Unplanned Pregnancy Advisory Service (NUPAS) website, or call them on 0333 004 6666 for help and advice
- Visit the MSI Reproductive Choices UK website. Alternatively, call them on 0345 300 8090 or email them at services@msichoices.org.uk

If you need help quickly

If you need help quickly you can contact these organisations:

- For medical advice contact NHS by dialling 111 24 hours a day, 365 days a year
- For help if you're under 18 contact Childline on 0800 1111
- For urgent emotional support contact the Samaritans on 08457 90 90 90

Glossary

Abortion

A procedure which prematurely ends a pregnancy through the removal or expulsion of the foetus. It can occur naturally (spontaneous abortion), but this is more commonly referred to as miscarriage. The term 'abortion' usually refers to the deliberate termination of an unwanted pregnancy (induced abortion).

The Abortion Act 1967

This act decriminalised abortion in cases where it had been certified by two doctors that certain grounds had been met, such as a serious risk to the mental or physical health of the pregnant woman.

Adoption

When a family becomes the legal guardians (adoptive parents) for a child who cannot be brought up by his or her biological parents. Couples who are infertile but wish to have a child look to adoption as an alternative. More recently, laws regarding adoption from overseas have become less strict.

Conception

The act of fertilisation, where an egg (ovum) joins together with a sperm (spermatozoon) to form an embryo or zygote. This term describes the moment a woman becomes pregnant.

Contraception

Anything which prevents conception, or pregnancy, from taking place. 'Barrier methods', such as condoms, work by stopping sperm from reaching an egg during intercourse and are also effective in preventing sexually transmitted infections (STIs). Hormonal methods such as the contraceptive pill change the way a woman's body works to prevent an egg from being fertilised. Emergency contraception, commonly known as the 'morning-after pill', is used after unprotected sex to prevent a fertilised egg from becoming implanted in the womb.

Down's Syndrome

Down's Syndrome is a genetic condition where a person is born with an extra chromosome that can cause mild to serious physical and developmental problems.

Embryo

Between day 14 and week eight of pregnancy the fertilised egg is referred to as an embryo. A zygote is simply the scientific term for the fertilised egg which is made by the joining of an egg (ovum) and sperm (spermatozoon). After the eighth week of pregnancy an unborn baby is referred to as a foetus.

Foetus

The unborn offspring of an animal or human being that has developed from an embryo.

Gestation

The development period of an embryo or foetus between conception and birth. As the exact date of conception in humans can be difficult to identify it is usually dated from the beginning of a woman's previous menstrual period.

Obstetricians and gynaecologists

A gynaecologist is a doctor who specialises in the health of the female reproductive system. An obstetrician is a doctor who specializes in pregnancy, childbirth, and a woman's reproductive system.

Pro-choice

Pro-choice supporters believe that it is a woman's right to choose whether or not to continue with a pregnancy. They also believe that the choice to have an abortion should be available to all.

Pro-life

Pro-life supporters believe that life begins at the moment of conception and think that an unborn child, foetus or embryo has the same rights as any other living person. They believe that the law should be changed so that abortion would be heavily restricted or outlawed in the UK.

Roe v. Wade

Roe v. Wade was a 1973 landmark decision by the US Supreme Court. The court ruled that a state law that banned abortions (except to save the life of the mother) was unconstitutional, effectively legalising the procedure across the United States. This decision was dramatically and controversially overturned in 2022 to the distress of many women and girls around the world.

Terminate

A term meaning 'to bring something to an end', an abortion is sometimes referred to as a termination.

Trimester

Human pregnancy is broken into three, 3-month stages. A trimester is one of those 3-month time periods.

Index